Hope for Nerds

The Life Story of Harold Eberle, Volume I

Harold R. Eberle
with Jim Bryson

Worldcast Publishing
Yakima, Washington, USA

Hope for Nerds
The Life Story of Harold Eberle, Part I

© 2014 by Harold R. Eberle
First printing, July 2014

Worldcast Publishing
P.O. Box 10653
Yakima, WA 98909-1653
(509) 248-5837
www.worldcastpublishing.com
office@worldcastpublishing.com

ISBN 978-1-882523-42-9
Cover by: Lynette Brannan
Final Edit: Amy Calkins
Sherrie StHiliare, the most graceful writer I know, also added her inspiration.

All biblical quotations are taken from the New American Standard Bible © 1977, The Lockman Foundation, La Habra, California 90631.

ALL RIGHTS RESERVED
No part of this publication may be reproduced, stored in a retrieval system, or transmitted in any form or by any means—electronic, mechanical, photocopy, recording, or otherwise—without the express prior permission of Worldcast Publishing Company, with the exception of brief excerpts in magazine articles and/or reviews.

Requests for translating into other languages should be addressed to Worldcast Publishing.

Printed in the United States of America

Glossary

Nerd

nərd \ (nûrd)
noun
informal

1. A person who behaves awkwardly around other people and usually has unstylish clothes, hair, etc.

2. A person who is boringly studious and very interested in technical subjects, science, etc.

See also: Harold Eberle

> A quirky loner who looks half his age, has tape wrapped around his broken horn-rimmed glasses, walks around with a pocket protector, and is oblivious to the fact that he is peculiar.

Table of Contents

Introduction 1

Chapter 1: Brave Heart, Bald Head 3
Chapter 2: The Baby of the Family 11
Chapter 3: Thoughts of a Seven-Year-Old 21
Chapter 4: We Were Catholics 27
Chapter 5: Whip that Goat! 35
Chapter 6: My Best Friend Was Furry 39
Chapter 7: Battle of Wounded Cheek 45
Chapter 8: Those Skinning-Dipping Girls 49
Chapter 9: Every Nerd Needs a Chemistry Set 53
Chapter 10: The Real Push-Up Champion! 57
Chapter 11: The Night I Broke Dad's Heart 63
Chapter 12: Escaping into the Wilds 69
Chapter 13: Living on Highway Pizza 75
Chapter 14: Training to be a Wildlife Biologist 81
Chapter 15: God Changed this Nerd 89

Other Books by Harold R. Eberle 95

Introduction

During 35+ years of public speaking, I have retold many stories from my youth. People sometimes ask more about those stories, so my friend, Jim Bryson, helped me compile them into this short book. Every story recounted here actually happened, but many years have passed, and stories develop as they are told over and over again. Therefore, be warned: These stories all have their roots in facts, but my memory is not immune to stretching some facts.

A caution to those who are faint of heart or weak of stomach. Being raised in Montana, my growing up years were very different than those of my metropolitan friends. I had a love for animals, nature, and hunting. Some of my exploits from that time seem crude and primitive, even to me now. It was a different time with different values.

Chapter One
Brave Heart, Bald Head

It all started one cold, drizzly afternoon. I was late getting out of school and running for the school bus as fast as my stick-thin legs would carry me. I bounded the three steps into the bus, and the crusty old driver—who had been waiting impatiently for me—yanked the smooth steel lever toward him, squeaking the door closed behind me. I stared down the aisle and realized with a sick feeling that the bus was packed. I froze.

As a first grader last to board the bus, my options for seating were severely limited—even lethal. All my friends were in the front rows, scrunched four to a seat, their tiny frames squeezed together for survival. They stared at me sympathetically, but that was about it. Two of my sisters—Rose and Patsy—also rode the bus, but they were paired up with friends and seemed to be doing their best to ignore me. Seating on the bus followed a strict, unwritten protocol, with only sixth-grade boys allowed in the back of the bus. The farther I ventured into their territory, the more dangerous things became.

The driver's voice hollered that I needed to find a seat NOW! I drove my rigid legs against the darkness swelling from the back. Wincing from the glares, I shuffled past every over-crowded seat, my heart pleading to every glaring face: Please let me sit; please let me live. Now I knew what the first explorers of the Amazon felt as they paddled into hostile territory with piranhas nipping at their paddles, waiting for one fatal tip of the canoe. One slip and I was bus meat.

Salvation appeared in the form of a sixth-grade boy I knew as Sam. He was hogging a seat all by himself while staring out the window. I'm not sure he noticed as I slid my rear end onto the sliver of seat not covered by his sprawling frame. Safe. I slowly released a deep breath, dropped my head, and drew myself inside, counting the minutes until home when I could escape from this cliff's ledge.

My relief was punctured by the snarl of another sixth-grade boy seated behind me.

"Hey little kid. What ya think yer doing?"

I didn't answer. I didn't move. Maybe he meant another little kid. I willed myself invisible. It didn't work. The sixth grader slugged me hard on the arm and snarled again, louder this time.

"Hey kid, I asked you something. Whacha doing here?"

The pain radiated from my soft muscles to the bones of my tiny frame.

Sam—the titan upon whose land I was trespassing—finally turned to take notice of me, and with a glance over his shoulder, my tormenter went silent. I melted with gratitude. Then sliding closer to me, Sam spoke in a warm tone and asked me my name.

"Harold," I said in a barely audible voice.

The eruption of laughter—something I would eventually get used to in life—made me drop my head again. What is it about the name Harold that invites ridicule? I don't know; it's the only name I've ever had. In the first grade, you don't have many choices. It's not like they wait until you're old enough to talk and then ask you what you'd like to be called. I'd have chosen Buck, Max, Shack, or Rip—anything that sounds big. But no, they don't give you a choice. They just give you a name and let you live with it.

The guffaws died out when Sam glanced back at the crowd. I was starting to feel safe at this point. I had a benefactor looking out for me and a corner of real estate that nobody had evicted me from. I slid the rest of my rear onto the seat, bowed my head, and waited for my bus stop. Life didn't get much better as a first grader sitting in the dark end of the bus.

Sam became friendly and chatty. He asked about my first-grade teacher, my sisters, and what I liked to do at home for fun. I told him how I liked to run through the woods and build forts. That seemed to pique his interest.

"So Harold, you must be pretty tough to run through the woods like that."

"Yeah," I said, feeling suddenly shy.

"So how tough are you?"

"Pretty tough I guess."

"Oh yeah? What makes you tough?"

I thought hard for a moment. "I didn't cry when I got slugged on the arm."

This made the guy behind me rise up. "I'll make you cry, punk."

"Hold it," said Sam, and the bully reluctantly dropped his arm, glaring at me instead. I was liking Sam more and more.

"So show me how tough you are," said Sam.

I couldn't think of anything, so I just hung my head and hoped for the conversation to be over. But Sam wasn't having any of it. He poked me in the ribs.

"Come on, Harold. Show me."

I guess it was the way he said "Harold" that made me want to impress him. Suddenly I had an idea! I took my fist and punched myself as hard as I could in the stomach and didn't let out a whimper. Surely this showed that I was tough. Sam laughed out loud, and on cue, so did the rest of the boys. I put my head back down unsure of what their reaction meant.

Sam jabbed me again.

"That's OK, I guess. But Harold, I want you to prove that you are really tough."

I had a flash of genius. I called to mind a gift I had: My hair was so fine that I could yank it out of my head without much effort. Without looking up, I muttered, "I can pull out my hair and not cry."

"You can pull out your hair without crying?" queried Sam.

"I can pull out my hair and not cry."

"Hey guys, you hear that? Little Harold here is a pretty tough guy. He can pull his hair out and not cry."

More laughs from the back of the bus. "Ah, he's lying," somebody shouted. "He can't do it," chimed in another.

"Oh, I bet he can," reassured Sam. "Come on, Harold, show me."

Determined to prove myself worthy, I took a handful of my fine, blonde hair, gave it a tug, and out it came, roots and all. I held up the trophy for all to see as my head dipped once more.

The boys cheered and congratulated me on this feat of toughness. Then Sam poked again.

"Betcha can't do it again."

"Betcha I can."

Hope for Nerds

With a grasp and a tug, I held up another tuft of hair. Cheers erupted. Now they saw how really tough I was. I lifted my chin high enough to receive the admiration on their faces. Not waiting for further provocation, I took another handful and yanked it out for all to see. The boys went wild, jumping on the seats and dancing in the aisle. Kids from the front made their way back to see the excitement. I glanced forward and caught Patsy's concerned eyes, but I didn't need her help. I had things under control. I was making new friends.

The sixth grader who had slugged me earlier leaned over and dared me to do it a fourth time. So I waved another fistful of hair before him, and he slapped the same shoulder that he had slugged. Without waiting for another invitation, I began to yank handful after handful of hair from my rapidly clearing scalp. My fear gone, I beamed into the faces of my former foes, each new tuft of emancipated hair bonding us closer.

"Harold, the mighty man!" they cheered.

The bus driver looked back at us through his mirror and bellowed for everyone to settle down. The bus went immediately silent. It was I who stirred them back into a frenzy by yanking another fistful of hair and tossing it into the air. My grin grew into a beaming smile as I swelled with pride. Soon the six-grade boys were leaning toward me and praising my courage. They all wanted to be my friend. They all wanted to know someone like me, to be like me—Harold the tough guy!

By the time my bus stop came, the seat upon which I sat was covered with thousands of silky blond hairs. I stood up and several fistfuls tumbled down off my shirt and pants. As I walked toward the front, I could feel some hair around my ears, but only a few patches of fuzz clinging to the top. My cowardly classmates looked at me with adoration.

As we stepped off of the bus, my sisters glanced my way but said nothing. I sensed their wonder at my manly feat, but I ignored them. As I planted my feet on solid ground, I waved triumphantly up at my new found friends. They cheered me from the windows, giving the thumbs up sign as the bus drove off in a plume of smoke. Not only had I survived my ride home with the sixth-grade boys, but I had shown myself a wonder. Harold the hero!

During the long, two-blocks-walk home, my sisters tried to interrogate me as to what had happened, but I remained mute, fueled by my new-found self-esteem. It wasn't until we mounted the porch steps and I saw my freakish reflection in the front window that my eyes opened to a new perspective. Mom would be on the other side of the door, horrified and desperate for answers. I tried to figure out what to tell her, but nothing came to mind. So I covered my head with my library book and walked in like I was balancing the book on my head. It didn't work. Mom snatched the book from my skull and jumped back with a start. Her face said it all. I tried to explain, but I just froze inside. All the courage I had garnered from the bus ride vanished with Mom's piercing gaze. I felt my eyes tearing up. Breaking from her eyes, I bolted for my bedroom. Mercifully, she let me go.

That evening at dinner, my hair and I were the topic of lively conversation. As the youngest of six, I was used to

Hope for Nerds

being at the bottom of the food chain, but that meal was especially brutal. It didn't help that my Dad was a barber. He kept staring at me but said nothing. Finally, someone suggested I had pulled my hair out to impress a girl. I never answered. What could I say? I didn't have a clue why I pulled my hair out. Taking my silence as confirmation, the story of Harold balding himself to impress a girl stuck and still circulates today among certain family members.

Although it took 50 years, I can now look back on that miserable day and chuckle. I still can't figure out why I pulled out my hair, but it certainly wasn't for a girl. I was in the first grade and still thought girls had cooties. I didn't even have the courage to talk to a girl, let alone try to impress one. And besides, what does pulling hair out have to do with impressing a girl? Today, as a middle-aged bald guy, I can state emphatically: Not much.

My hair eventually grew back, but in recent years it has receded to the fashion I introduced in first grade. Actually, being bald is not so bad. I don't have to pay a barber to do what my Dad used to do for free. And I don't have to pull my hair behind my head with a hair tie like some of my ex-hippie friends. But probably the best thing about being bald is that I get to tell everyone I'm bald because God keeps kissing me on the top of my head. He thinks I'm cute.

That's better than a bus ride with sixth-grade goons any day!

Chapter Two
The Baby of the Family

I was the youngest of six kids.

Eram infantem. Ego sum infantem. Ego semper esse infantem.

I was the baby. I am the baby. I will always be the baby.

That means I had footie pajamas until I was eight.

To make matters worse, my parents enrolled me into kindergarten when I was four. I'm sure this made me the youngest and smallest kid in the school system. Maybe they figured I'd be more at home that way—still the runt of the litter. Instead, it was like hanging a sign on my back: WHACK THE LITTLE KID! FREE KICKS!

By the second grade, I was having difficulty talking—go figure—so the school put me in speech therapy class. Oh sure, I could speak all right, just not loud enough for anybody to hear, especially adults…or older kids…or anybody bigger than me…which was pretty much everybody. These days, I can preach up a storm, but back then I was just too scared to speak. It might have had something to do with the fact that whenever I did open my mouth, a sibling was there to close it for me. I'll tell you, folks: Life ain't easy for the tiniest potato in the sack.

Hope for Nerds

Fern, my oldest sister, was the perfect child of the family. Still is, as a matter of fact. She got straight A's in school, won praise and honors from all her teachers, helped Mom around the house, and treated her baby brother the way he deserved to be treated. Fern is the most giving person I have ever known. (Fern, if you are reading this, I think you're great!)

Sadly, when you are the only half-pint in a milk box of gallon jugs, things don't always go right with your siblings. One day, Fern crept up from behind, grabbed my ribs, and started tickling me mercilessly. As I laughed and tried to escape her onslaught, I jumped up hard, cracking her chin with my head. I heard the crunch, and she let go immediately, falling back in pain. Stifling her tears, she got to her feet and staggered to her bedroom, holding her jaw and her body heaving the way people do when they can't cry out loud. I heard her bedroom door slam and sobs erupt. I slumped to the floor in bewilderment.

I wanted to run into her room, plead my case, tell her I was sorry. But I couldn't. So I just sat on the floor outside her bedroom, listening to her anguish. Even if the words could have left my lips, I'm not sure what I would have said. We were not a family that spoke our feelings. We didn't have Dr. Phil on TV. Instead, we had *Gunsmoke*, *Rawhide*, and *Dragnet* ("Just the facts, ma'am."). We didn't share our hearts like people do today. I didn't know how to say "Fern, I'm sorry. Please forgive me." I'm sure she understood it was an accident, but I'm not sure she understood how badly I felt. We never spoke of it. Like I said, she was perfect.

Of course, not all my siblings were perfect. I shared

The Baby of the Family

a bedroom with my two big brothers: Jim and Claude. (I always thought Claude was a funny name. Funnier than Harold. Nothing funny about Harold.)

When Claude and I were small, we shared a single bed, although shared is a relative term, meaning it depends on which relative is doing the sharing. Being older, Claude drew an imaginary line down the middle of our bed and demanded that I keep to my side. Trouble was, his half seemed to take up most of my half. I wasn't good at fractions in those days, but I knew when I was getting the worst of a deal. I just didn't know what to do about it. I didn't like conflict—mostly because I didn't like losing, and besides, who picks a fight with a guy named Claude? So I adapted like any shrimp in the Pacific Ocean would and learned to survive on the edge. Which is lousy for a little kid but a great skill for a future iconoclast preacher. Even if his parents did name him…ah, forget it.

Jim and Claude were able to pull some mean tricks on me. There wasn't much to do around the house, so little brother had to suffice for entertainment.

One evening, Jim and Claude offered me 10 cents to trade beds with the dog for the night. I wasn't too keen on sleeping in the dog's bed—hair and fleas made me itch—but when your older brothers make you an offer, it's not really a choice, and it's not about the money. You just do it, and if you get paid, so much the better. I think the dog got a good night's sleep that evening; I know I didn't. Come to think of it, I never got the dime either.

Because they were older, my brothers got to stay up later than me, which meant I was usually sound asleep when they came to bed. One miserable evening, after putting on their pajamas and moving up the clock, they shook me awake and shouted: "Harold, get up. It's time for school. You're late!" I jumped out of bed, threw on my clothes, and rushed to the breakfast table fearing the worst. I sat there for a long time, wondering where everyone was. Finally, I looked at the kitchen clock, figured out what the big hand and little hand were saying, and knew I'd been had. Frustrated and embarrassed, I slipped back to the bedroom where Jim and Claude were snickering. They played that joke on me more than once. I guess I was kinda slow back then, but I was never late for school.

Despite the pranks they played on me, having big brothers had advantages. My oldest brother, Jim, was the smartest, bravest brother any kid ever had. He knew things no one else knew. He even taught me how to focus the sunlight with a magnifying glass, then burn ants until they spewed out an awesome blue-green smoke, then crinkled into a black ash pile.

When Jim said something, everyone listened —especially me. Sometimes Mom called him "Samson" because he was so strong. Today, as a parent myself, I suspect it was also her way to get him to do chores.

Jim liked being the big brother; he was good at it, but he had a mean streak. When I did something to make him mad—which could be anything—he would grumble, "Come here, Harold. I'm gonna hit you, and the longer you take to get here, the harder you're gonna get hit."

I realize that by today's standards this sounds like child abuse. And maybe it was. But I loved Jim and he

The Baby of the Family

loved me. We simply lived in different times back then, and I did get to be pretty quick on my feet.

One day, Jim let me come with him into the woods across the road. I was ecstatic, because I was the shortest rope on the Goodyear Blimp and he rarely let me accompany him anywhere; usually it was Claude who got to go. This morning, however, Jim had a special job only I could fulfill. Me! Harold! I would have charged hell with a squirt gun to prove myself worthy.

Turned out Jim wanted to build a snare, one that would catch bad guys. We'd had some thievery around our neighborhood, and Jim figured he'd catch a few of the creeps hiding out in our woods and turn them over to the police. Or maybe just thrash them within an inch of their lives and tell them never to be in these parts again. Jim was tough. Nobody messed with Jim. Not even bad guys.

Deep in the woods, Jim found the perfect tree and lassoed the end of a long branch, pulling it to the ground like a giant bow. On the other end of the big rope, he tied a noose wide enough for a man's foot, securing it with a smaller rope staked to the ground. Then he dug a narrow hole, laying a trigger stick across the hole and the noose around it. He covered the whole thing with leaves. The trigger stick controlled the smaller rope, so when a bad guy stepped on the trigger stick, it would break and release the bent branch to spring back to its upright position, hopefully snatching the leg of the criminal in the noose and yanking him upside down about 6 feet in the air—the ideal position for interrogation. "So what did you do with the Widow Larson's chickens last week?" It was an amazing plan, and as I watched Jim work this technological miracle, I wondered what my part would be, the job that only I could do, my special purpose.

After the trap was set, Jim hollered, "Harold, get over here."

True to my conditioning, I sprinted toward him, giving a wide berth to the trap area.

"No," growled Jim. "Not that way. Over here." His finger outlined a path across the leaves covering the noose.

Now, I may have been the youngest, but I wasn't the dumbest. I knew what this contraption was for. I'd seen snares in hunting books, but I also knew what to expect if I didn't instantly obey Jim's command. So I changed course as directed, gliding my 42-pound frame as lightly as possible across the noose.

It didn't spring.

I stifled my smile. Jim muttered some words and examined the contraption. After checking everything out, he had me back up and come toward the noose again, walking slowly this time. I willed myself to levitate like I'd read in fairy tales, and it must have worked, because the trap still didn't spring.

Jim muttered some more, threw down his tools, and began to fiddle with every moving part. Things normally came easy to him, so he could quickly become frustrated when they didn't. While I stood back to watch, fearing his wrath as he double-checked each component, he finally stomped his foot into the leaves where the noose was hidden. Sure enough, it sprang! His leg was yanked out from under him and before he could finish hollering, up into the air he went, hanging upside down like a deer carcass waiting for the butcher.

Swinging back and forth, he finally yelled: "HAROLD! Get Mom!"

I stood transfixed. Jim, my big brother, my hero, our Samson, needed my help! Sure, he was trussed up like a Christmas goose and spinning furiously, but certainly he'd find a way to get out of this. All I had to do was wait and watch and...

"Harold, get Mom NOW!"

I came out of my trance. Sprinting furiously over fallen logs and sharp rocks, I kept thinking how cool it was that Jim was hanging upside down in a tree. I mean, he was smart enough to build a snare that actually worked. My big brother did that! I thought about getting my friends and showing them what Jim built. They'd all be amazed, too. But...that would mean leaving him there longer, and he didn't seem too keen on being up there in the first place. So I made the wise decision to forgo showing Jim off and got Mom instead, but by the time I led her back to the tree, Jim had already freed himself just like Samson would have done. I waited for him to reset the trap and try again, but he just shook his head and walked off. I guess even Jim had tough days.

Besides building traps, Jim also got to do all the cool stuff around the house. He even got to use Dad's power tools: the circular saw that threw blue sparks, the sander that could tame the roughest board, and the electric drill. I loved watching that drill in action. After spending hours with my puny hand-crank drill making holes through a pine board, I was amazed at what Dad and Jim could do with a one-second blast of the power drill.

One day I found myself sitting on the kitchen floor watching Jim drill holes in metal cabinet hinges. It was tough work because the drill bit was getting dull, but he was almost done and didn't want to stop to change it. Instead, he leaned harder on the drill. An instant later, the bit slipped off the metal and went straight into his calf muscle. To make matters worse, the drill was locked on so it kept spinning. Funny what a dull bit can do to soft flesh. Well…not so funny, but you have to admit that it was cool.

Jim's blood gushed into a spreading pool on the linoleum floor. Grimacing ever so slightly, he pulled the drill out of his leg and bound the seeping hole with a dish towel, then surveyed the wound with a detached air of amusement. While I wiped up the bloody floor, Jim casually rinsed the drill bit and went right back to working on the metal hinges. He never whimpered; he never cried. He was tough. He was my big brother.

Although Jim often got the best of me, the great equalizer in our family was Dad. One summer evening after dinner, as the crickets sang, I heard Dad goofing around with Jim and Claude on the front lawn. I ran out, then sat on the porch steps watching from a distance. I didn't dare get any closer. The three of them were getting rough, laughing and slapping and punching in mock battle—one of the few times they were allowed to challenge Dad. I wanted to join in but figured I'd either get hurt or manage to hurt Jim or Claude, which meant I'd get hurt later. There really weren't any better options, so I stayed put.

Finally, Dad noticed me. While holding Jim and Claude down with one arm and pointing with the other, he hollered, "Harold, under the trash cans, get me a handful of those slugs." I brought the slimy creatures over to him, and to my delight, he slid them down Jim and Claude's pants. They howled and thrashed in vain as Dad kept them pinned against the cool grass. For me, it was a clash of titans. I glowed on the inside but didn't dare crack a smile. Dad finally let my tormentor-heroes loose, and they ran into the house, squealing and writhing like scolded puppies.

I stayed close to Dad for the rest of the evening and thought about how there was some fairness in the world after all. Even if it did come from the underside of a trash can.

Chapter Three
Thoughts of a Seven-Year Old

We were poor, but so was everybody else in our world, so we didn't know we were poor. Dad was a minimalist way before the environmental movement made it popular to get by on as little as possible. For a while we only owned a Volkswagen bug, which all eight of us had to fit in when we went to church on Sundays. It was fine until Dad started picking up an old crippled man who needed a ride to church. We left a small carbon footprint.

Dad worked five days a week as a barber and took off Sunday and Monday. Of course, his off-days simply meant a change in work. We had some land and a few goats and chickens, so there were always chores for all of us to do.

I will admit I had it easiest because I was the baby. Even at seven years old, however, I spent many days working on the pile of used lumber in front of the chicken coup. I sorted the boards by length, stacked them, and pulled out any nails that were stuck in them. I learned the economy of recycling as Dad reused the boards and nails on other projects. We threw little away.

Sometimes I got help from a neighbor boy named Billy. He generally avoided our house on work days because he knew Dad would assign him a job too. "You play here, you work here, Billy." But sometimes Billy was desperate enough for a playmate that he would help me finish my chores so we could do something together. Our favorite game was croquet—using a mallet to hit wooden balls through a course of steel hoops. The first one to hit his ball through to the end wins. Billy wasn't very good at croquet, which is probably why he cheated when he thought I wasn't looking. I never said anything about it, but it bothered me.

Billy's family wasn't like mine. His father and mother fought a lot. His dad was mean, and I could see he didn't like Billy's mom all that much. Billy's dad worked nights at some job I never understood, and he slept during the day. This meant whenever we played at Billy's house we were supposed to be quiet. But we were kids. It didn't help that Billy's bedroom was next to his parents' room. Billy's dad could yell louder than anybody I'd ever heard.

Billy's bed was under a window that had a wooden sill extending a couple inches out from the wall. The first time I was in his room, I noticed teeth marks and splinters along the length of the window sill; much of the wood was chewed away. I knew Billy didn't have any pets—his dad wouldn't allow it—so it had to be Billy. I imagined him staring out the window as his parents fought, chewing on the wooden sill and dreaming of someplace far away where people didn't yell. Even though I was just a kid, I knew Billy was troubled. I wondered if he would end up in jail when he grew up.

One day I nearly closed the window on our friendship. I caught him cheating again—this time taking outrageous liberties with our game—and it pushed me over an edge I didn't know I had. I screamed and shoved him down into the grass. Billy looked shocked at the quiet kid suddenly going ballistic. I didn't care. Taking advantage of his prone position, I grabbed his ear and twisted it as hard as I could, all the while yelling invectives against his cheating. I pulled so hard I thought his ear would come off. Finally, Billy screamed and recovered his legs, making a dash for the safety of his own house while I chased him to my property line and warned him loudly against ever crossing it again. After he was out of view, I stopped and wondered what had happened to me. I'd never gotten angry like that before; it scared me. What was I capable of doing when I lost my temper? I couldn't remember anyone in my family ever getting that mad.

We rarely raised our voices in our home. Even when my brothers picked on me, it was done quietly. "Come here, Harold, or else," could be delivered with just as much venom in a whisper as in a shout. That's probably where I learned that when your conviction is firm, you don't have to yell.

Our religious commitment taught us to be reserved. We were devout Catholics. In the center of our living room was a table set up like a shrine with a Bible, a candle, and a statue of the Blessed Virgin Mary, who remained piously mute. At Mass, which we attended regularly, the priests rarely raised their voices.

Today I am glad we were Catholics. Some people who were raised Catholic grow up and resent their upbringing. They judge their Catholic experience as nothing more than ritual and rules. It was never like that for me. Even though

Hope for Nerds

I left the Catholic Church at 17, I cherished my times of communion with God in silent buildings highlighted with candles, stained glass, and incense. That is where I first came to know God.

Church taught me some interesting things, though often not the lessons my teachers intended. On Saturdays during long, hot summers, we parish children endured Catechism classes in the windowless basement of our church building. The lay teachers tried their best, but I mostly remember chaos among disinterested kids.

One Saturday, I heard my teacher say something that cut through the sweltering din. She quoted the words of Jesus: "Whoever says to this mountain, 'Be taken up and cast into the sea,' and does not doubt in his heart, but believes that what he says is going to happen, it will be granted him." This idea staggered me. I could move mountains? Objects would obey me? I could make things happen just by believing? I thought of Billy and Dad and all the struggling people I could help with this ability. If I only believed enough, Dad could have more money and stop working so hard. Billy's dad could quit his night job, and maybe he wouldn't yell at Billy so much. I could help mom and my brothers and sisters have the things they always wanted. Oh, the endless possibilities!

As soon as I got home, I had to put my faith to work bending the laws of the universe. I figured I'd start with something simple and build up to more complex feats as my skills grew. I dashed to my room and searched through my stash of secret stuff. See, when you have five brothers and sisters pushing you to the bottom of the totem pole, you learn to horde some stuff as a hedge against extinction.

Thoughts of a Seven-Year Old

My fingers wrapped around one of my best treasures: a metal Band-Aid box with a hinged lid. It was the size of a cigarette pack (something I only saw in Billy's house). I got the idea to use my faith to make the box float. Besides being a future theologian, I was also a budding chemist, so into the Band-Aid box I mixed a potion concocted from Mom's kitchen spices and dirt from the goat pen. I figured that my mix of secret stuff combined with mountain-mover faith would make the Band-Aid container hover in mid-air. If I could make a metal box float, I could change the world. At least that was my plan.

I took the precious container to the backyard, set it gingerly on the ground, and closed my eyes, pushing aside all doubts. I prayed, keeping my eyes closed long enough for the special compound and my faith to work. When I opened my eyes, I just knew the Band-Aid container would be floating and I would be famous.

It wasn't floating.

So I shut my eyes tighter and counted the seconds, my faith growing with every tick. After a few minutes, I started to nod off, so I figured enough time had passed. When I opened my eyes again, I looked up to where I expected the box to be hovering, but it wasn't there. Did it rise too high? No. It was still on the ground where I'd left it. Maybe I wasn't getting this right. Did Jesus say I had to close my eyes? Did He say anything about how to make the mountain move? No, He didn't. He just said you could move it. Still, I decided to give it some more time while I walked around the house clearing my mind of any weak thoughts. Certain I had hit on the correct alchemy at last, I returned to the launching pad of my faith only to find the metal box still resting on the mineral-rich ground that had spawned it.

Something was wrong. I prayed again—more fervently. Yet when I looked, the box hadn't moved. Instead, something moved in me—a deep sadness that I'd never experienced before. You see, I lived in a world of certainty. When Dad said he was coming home, he came home. When Mom said dinner was on the table, we ate. When Fern said "Smell this flower, Harold," it smelled good. When Jim said "Get over here, Harold, or else," I got over there. Most certain of all, however, were the words of my religion teachers, for they had the words of God, and they had just taught me something that didn't work. At seven years old, I felt betrayed. I was disillusioned in a way that reached deep into my heart. Someone had lied to me. I wasn't sure who it was, but that lie lodged deep in my soul.

Then I thought about Billy, how he must feel lied to everyday—disillusioned and cheated most of the time. He probably dreamed of better things while chewing that window sill, pretending to be far away. Maybe that's why he liked our house. It was a safe place, as far as his little legs could carry him.

The next week, Billy came over and we didn't say much. He just lent a hand while I stacked wood and pulled nails. Later, we played croquet, and while he cheated again, I didn't say anything this time.

I just let him win.

Chapter Four
We Were Catholics

At the end of my second grade year, our family moved from Bothell, Washington to Helena, Montana, where all of us kids began attending a private Catholic school. After two years in public school, this was quite a culture shock. I thought the teachers in the public school were strict, but they were nothing compared to the nuns who ran this new place. These ladies had a firm belief that kids were prone to trouble and required a strong hand to stay out of mischief.

One teacher, Sister Rose Marie, was the patron saint for tough love, minus the love part. She towered over us, casting a cold shadow upon our impressionable souls. Her weathered cheeks wobbled as she spoke, and her beady eyes missed nothing. I'd read about giant trolls in my library books. Looming before me was their matriarch wrapped in starched black and white linens. One look from her, and I got the message quick: "Do not mess with this brute!" Even the devil was afraid of her.

Unfortunately, not everyone learned as fast.

Gary was new to the school just like me. I didn't know him well, but I could tell he was the trouble-making type. He had a slick grin, chewed gum over sour breath, and made sly comments behind Sister's back, comparing her to large furry mammals and other territorial beasts. While the rest of us respectfully called her "Sister," Gary referred to her as "the penguin." His shocking antics kept us in stitches, but we were terrified to laugh out loud. To our amazement, Sister seemed to take no notice of Gary's attitude.

As the days went by, Gary grew bolder and louder, but Sister continued to ignore him. Finally, just as we were beginning to doubt her ability to hear, Gary leaned back, smirked, and smarted off directly to Sister's face, breaking his own record for verbal insolence. I knew it was a mistake. Oh, poor Gary.

The words had no sooner left his grinning lips when Sister Rose Marie stopped her lesson, walked up, and stood directly over Gary. She surveyed him blankly for a moment, freezing the grin on his face. Then she let out a long breath, drew back her gnarled hand, and cracked him across the mouth so violently his neck twisted before snapping back like a rubber doll. We watched in awe as Gary gasped out a scream, stuck a finger in his mouth, and spit out two bloody teeth. No one said another word after that. Not that day. Not ever. Not even Gary.

Of course, not all the Sisters were as severe as Sister Rose Marie. Some were actually fun to be around. They enjoyed playing with us at recess and would make jokes in class to liven things up. I guess they loved kids, and because they couldn't have any of their own, we were their children.

The summer of my fourth grade, I was given the responsibility of maintaining the half-acre lawn at the convent where the sisters lived. This was a huge privilege for the baby of the family. I even got to use a power mower—something that never happened at home. In their instructions to me, the sisters made it clear they were counting on me to keep their lawn looking pristine while they were away for summer training. They were putting their complete trust and confidence in me. Of course, they were women of great faith.

For the first month, I diligently mowed and watered, weeded and trimmed, and was proud of how everything looked. But as the days ran into weeks, I got involved in more interesting activities around home and…well, I sort of forgot about the sisters and their lawn.

Then one lazy afternoon toward the end of summer, I found myself walking past a neighbor's lawn, admiring its deep green, and it hit me like a bale of hay: I was in deep, deep do-do. I ran the whole way to the convent, praying the lawn was okay. But this was summer—dry months in Montana. Without constant watering, grass withered and died, and the convent lawn was no exception. In sheer panic, I unrolled the hose and started a massive watering, willing the dead grass to life. But at the end of the day, I had nothing for my efforts but rivers of mud flowing between clumps of high brown stalks. Although I went back every day for a week and labored for resurrection, the lawn did not return by the time the sisters did. Sadly, I knew I'd disappointed them and would never be put in charge of the lawn again.

I must have had some redeeming qualities, however, for the following year the janitor (custodian these days) gave me an even more important job than lawn boy—one that paid a nickel a day. I was placed in charge of emptying all the classroom garbage cans after school. This meant I was the only kid allowed in the school building after hours. You better believe I let all my friends know about my elevated status, waving to them from inside whenever I could catch their eye. Of course, they tried to get me to let them in, but I never did. Guess a guy learns something from his past mistakes. This was one job I wasn't going to screw up.

Other than killing grass and collecting trash, being a good Catholic boy also meant I took my turn as an altar boy. My brothers Jim and Claude were already altar boys, and it thrilled me to follow in their footsteps. Essentially, an altar boy's job was to help the priest during Mass. We lit candles, filled wine decanters and water basins, rang bells at the appointed times, responded to the priest in Latin during Mass, helped serve communion, and cleaned up after everyone left. Some of the boys did the job for the attention it garnered, and others had a great interest in the leftover wine after the Mass, but for me, it was a chance to serve God and help the priests, whom I revered.

For two months, Claude helped me learn all the Latin I would need. Just before we fell asleep each night, he would lie in the top bunk and recite the Latin phrases while I repeated them from the bottom bunk. I finally had all the sentences memorized, although I did not know what they meant. Still, I loved hearing the priest speak Latin during Mass. It sounded mystical to me, like the language God would speak in Heaven.

I was the smallest altar boy my parish had ever seen. In my regal black and white robes, sporting a mop of fine, blonde hair, I was a hit with the older ladies. They seemed to enjoy watching this little nerd carry out his duties, waiting to see if he would come in on cue.

People had good reason to wonder about me. Staying awake in the warm, stuffy church was a challenge during long stretches of the Mass when an altar boy had little to do. One day as I sat waiting my turn with the bell, the priest droned on and on in that mystical language. I felt my mind filling with sand. Smoke rose from the incense pots as my eyelids drifted shut and my head slumped forward. The melodic Latin coming from the priest was now coming from Claude who wore vestments of blue denim and threw holy water in my face, laughing and winding the hands of a giant alarm clock backwards while whispering my name: "Harold...Harold....wake up."

Who was calling me? I knew it couldn't be God; He spoke Latin.

Finally, the voice said sharply, "HAROLD!" I jerked awake and started furiously ringing my bell, my ears filled with the sudden assault. Finally alert now, I saw the priest smiling at me. Embarrassed, I dropped my bell and thought about bolting. Then I looked out into the congregation and saw they were smiling too. So I picked up my bell, grinning sheepishly, and Mass continued, a bit brighter, it seemed, then before my nap.

Throughout the school year all of us students had to attend Mass every day. We were raised in the church, educated in the church, and consequently, our friendships grew from the church.

Hope for Nerds

One of my best friends was Ramon. He was from Cuba. Around 1960, thousands of parents in Cuba sent their children to the United States to escape the poverty and religious oppression that Fidel Castro was imposing. These children were not really orphans because they still had parents back in Cuba, but about 100 of them lived at the Roman Catholic orphanage located on the outskirts of our town. Ramon was one of them. We were friends, even though he did not speak much English during his first year at school.

After two years, Ramon was formally adopted into a local family from our church because someone decided his parents would never make it to the U.S. He was sad about being forever separated from his birth family, but he seemed to like his new home and understood it was for the better. His new family also adopted Ramon's younger cousin, who was the same age as their natural son. These two boys became close companions while Ramon remained the outsider.

Then one day it all went terribly wrong. The two younger boys—both seven years old—went out to a field and crawled into a dark concrete cavity that was built to house irrigation equipment. The boys had often played there, but this time they brought a coffee can of gasoline and matches, intending to illuminate the space. The explosion was heard for a quarter mile.

Ramon reacted to the tragedy by growing even more distant, even from me. He stopped talking to people and was eventually sent off to a different school in the hopes that a fresh start would help him heal. I never heard from him after that. To this day, I miss him and hope to see him again.

I did hear about Gary, the student who had two teeth smacked out of his mouth at school. It was not until about 30 years later, when I was a school bus driver for a few months and Gary's teenage son, Joshua, road my bus. Joshua was the bus clown, and he could keep the whole bus load of kids laughing. I tried not to encourage his antics, but he was hilarious. It was not until after several weeks that I found out he was Gary's son. I found out because talk went around the bus one day that Josh's dad had committed suicide. After checking into it, I learned his dad was the same Gary who had spit out two teeth in third grade.

Josh was a lot quieter for the rest of that school year.

Chapter Five
Whip that Goat!

Right before I started junior high school, we moved to a new house in the country. We now had a small farm with chickens, a cow or two, and some goats. Being a farm kid, it was my job to feed the chickens every morning and evening. That was okay; I liked chickens, especially for dinner on Sundays.

But there was one serious problem. In order to get to the chicken coop, I had to go through the goat corral, and we had a mean goat in there who didn't like me. He was big and ugly with 20-inch long curved horns. Dried manure clung to his straggly hair, and his evil goat-eyes pierced straight into my soul. He knew I was a nerd. He hated nerds.

Every morning, I woke up trying to figure out how to sneak into the goat corral, slip past that stupid goat, and get to the chicken coup. Most mornings I crept out of the house as quietly as possible. Then I'd sneak across the backyard, concealing my advancement by moving from bush to tree. When I finally reached the corral, I had to decide whether to open the rusty gate and slip through or just climb over the fence and hope for the best. It didn't really matter though, because that stupid goat with 20-inch long horns would always be waiting. I think he got up early just for me.

The instant my feet landed on goat territory, he'd churn his hooves and charge. As fast as my scrawny legs flew, I could only get halfway across the corral before he caught me and start ramming my backside with his horns. I was a little guy and he was a big, stupid goat. It hurt. I hated that goat.

Sometimes he knocked me into the ground, and you can imagine what was mixed in the dirt of the goat corral. It filled my mouth when I screamed. It was gross. And while I was down, he'd ram me some more as I crawled toward the chickens. It sickened me knowing I was going to school covered in that goat's manure—the final insult. I swear I could hear that goat snickering.

I ran from that goat every day, before and after school, month after month, for hundreds of years (okay, that part is exaggerated). Did I mention that I hated that goat? And he hated me!

One morning my dad was home working in the barn. I didn't want him to see what I lived with every day, so I redoubled my efforts at stealth, sneaking from bush to tree like a ninja nerd. By the time I made it to the corral gate, the goat was nowhere to be seen. Maybe he died? Visions of goat burgers smoking on the grill lifted my spirit. This might be a good day after all.

I stepped hopefully through the gate. The goat shot out from behind his goat house and charged me full-force, striking my gut and driving me to the ground with obvious delight. All the air in my lungs evacuated into

Whip that Goat!

a guttural scream. He kept pounding me as I crawled toward the chicken coop and safety. A lifetime of anguish erupted in my heart. We made a ghastly racket; my rage and the goat's snickering.

It was then that a light broke through from heaven.

Dad stepped out of the barn to see what all the commotion was. To my amazement, the goat backed away from me and stood motionless, staring at Dad. I hoisted myself unto my shaky legs, hung my head, and started toward the chickens. Then Dad disappeared into the barn and the stupid goat charged me again, ramming me in the stomach and knocking me down just like before. I don't know what hurt worse—the 20-inch horns or being abandoned by Dad.

From my prone position, I grabbed fistfuls of rancid soil and stared at the barn door as the goat continued using me for battering practice. Dad reappeared a moment later, this time wielding a light chain about five feet long. The goat stopped ramming me and backed away just like before. Dad walked over to where I lay, dropped the chain in my hand, and walked off. "What's this?" As Dad turned back toward the barn, that stupid goat charged me again, but right before that goat reached me, Dad turned and yelled, "Whip him!"

"Whip him?" I jumped to my feet and swung the chain through the air in a tight arc. Just as that stupid goat was ready to ram me, I cracked it across his back, stunning him motionless. I murmured a note of amazement. Dad yelled, "Whip him again!" So I cracked that goat across his flank, and to my delight, he ran to the far corner of the corral and cowered. Then Dad uttered his final epitaph, "Have some fun, boy!"

I chased that stupid goat around the corral, whipping him and screaming like a banshee while Dad looked on grinning.

That was one of the best days of my life. I didn't feel like such a nerd after that. I would meet many other goats in my life, but nothing ever felt so satisfying as taming that first one. And the stupid goat with 5-inch long horns never looked cross at me or any other nerd ever again.

Chapter Six
My Best Friend Was Furry

I love dogs. I had several throughout my growing years, but my favorite was Alex. He was a medium-sized, furry mutt that we got from the dog pound (called an animal shelter today). He was equal parts chow, shepherd, malamute, hound, and woolly mammoth. Alex was warm, wild, and eager. He'd go anywhere; he'd attack anything; he was always ready for adventure. Alex was 100% fun. He was my best friend.

Behind our pasture was a dairy farm surrounded by acres of grassland and brush with an icy creek running through it. Alex and I spent many days exploring that land. He was my scout; I was the fearless hunter, Daniel Boon or Davie Crockett.

Of course, my hunting required some improvisation, as I was too young for a gun in those days. So Alex and I usually hunted with a homemade bow and arrow. It was powerful but wildly inaccurate. Not surprising, I rarely hit anything that I aimed at, but we had fun. I used to take aim at gophers that stood in front of their holes wondering who these intruders were—one two-footed and the other four. Gophers were dimwitted and fat—my favorite targets. Later in life, I would grow to develop a culinary affinity for the tender little critters. For now, they simply made tempting targets, even if they could still evade my clumsy advances. Alex loved chasing them, but they could duck underground too quickly for him. Still, gophers were a pest to the farmers in our area, so we were glad to harass them even if we couldn't bring a trophy home.

One day, I actually killed a gopher, but not in the way I had planned. In fact, he hardly flinched as my crude arrow flew harmlessly past his head. His nonchalance was especially galling because that was the only arrow I had that day, plus I hadn't taught Alex to retrieve yet. In frustration, I hurled my bow at the creature and miraculously entangled him in the string. Alex came bounding along and finished him off before the gopher could free himself. So we bagged our first gopher that day, not with my bow and arrow but with my bow and dog.

Of course, things didn't always go smoothly for me and Alex. One hot summer day when the water was low, we raced along the creek bed, leaping between stones and looking for fish in eddy pools. Alex was running full speed—the only speed he knew—when his front paw stepped on a stick lying across a rock. The stick jutted up and stuck him hard in the belly. He'd been running so fast that the stick drilled right into him. His yelp sent chills down my spine.

Poor Alex couldn't walk, so I gathered up his furry mass and lugged him over a mile home. He whimpered the whole way and so did I. My family rarely took our animals to the veterinarian, but Dad saw how torn up I was and let me take Alex. Doc Ellis treated the wound and gave us some pills, showing us how to get a reluctant dog to swallow them.

My Best Friend Was Furry

Back home, Alex's rear leg swelled up with an infection. He lay around the house for two weeks, and if I tried to pet him, he'd whimper and then lick my hand with his dry tongue. My dog was tough, though. He finally started walking again, wincing in pain at first. Happily, we were soon back to running the creek at full speed. I expected Alex to be a bit tentative about where he stepped, but if anything, he was even wilder.

Aside from gophers, Alex and I also encountered a few skunks during our hunting trips. The poor dog always got the worst of the encounter, however. He would get sprayed and smell so badly he'd have to sleep by himself outside for a week. He didn't seem to mind, though. If anything, he seemed pleased with himself.

Anything gets better with practice, and I soon began to skillfully hunt skunks with my bow and arrow. Skunks were bigger targets than gophers, and not as fast, so I could get closer to them. In the field behind our property, the dairy owners had a pit where they tossed dead cows to rot. After dark, the nocturnal skunks would emerge from their dens and crawl into those bloated carcasses for a tasty meal. I would hide out near the pit, and if I could stand the smell long enough, a skunk or two would mosey along, and I would shoot it with my much-improved bow and arrow. The best part about hitting a skunk was how it would empty its scent bag, mingling with the smell of the decayed corpses and producing a stench so bad that I wanted to puke. Don't ask me why I liked that; I'm not sure.

One time, instead of Alex getting sprayed, it was me. Skunk revenge, I guess. I smelled so badly my school

Hope for Nerds

teacher made me sit by myself in the back of the class.

Sitting in my backyard one night, scanning the horizon for predators and protecting the home front, I saw a skunk trekking across the field about 20 yards away—just outside my range. Still, I took a shot but only managed to wound him. One of my best arrows dragging from its side, the skunk hobbled into the trailer court next to our property, and I gave chase. But before I could catch up to it to retrieve my prized arrow, the skunk crawled under a trailer and quietly died. I knew it was dead because, as usual, it emptied its scent bag. The sudden stench stopped me in my tracks, and my better judgment told me not to go any closer. I'm glad I listened. A moment later, three people burst out of the trailer, choking and crying and gasping for air. I doubt they saw me through their tears. I watched from the shadows for a while and then quietly slipped away. I never did tell another soul what happened until now. So folks, if you are reading this, I'm sorry about the skunk. I didn't plan for it to die under your trailer. Oh, and if you don't mind, I'd appreciate having my arrow back.

One summer day my family went on a trip to the mountains, and best of all, Alex came along. We were fishing in a little creek when Alex found a porcupine minding its own business and trying to scurry away. Naturally, Alex lunged for it. Unfortunately, that porcupine had plans that didn't involve becoming my dog's next meal, so he swung his tail and smacked my crazed canine across the nose and deep into his gapping mouth. Oh, the howl that Alex made as his assailant fled in victory. Score that one: Porcupine 1, Dog 0.

My Best Friend Was Furry

Alerted by his agonizing cries, we all came running. Alex's face looked like mom's pin cushion. Dad said we had to get the quills out before they got infected, so with me holding on to his 800 pound writhing mass, Dad yanked a few of the larger quills from Alex's poor nose by hand. But it was too hard to get the rest out without pliers, especially the quills inside his mouth. So we made the long drive back home while my furry buddy lay in the back of the van, wincing and whining with each bump. I felt every bump too.

When we got home, a neighbor came over to help Dad pull out the rest of the quills. He forced Alex's mouth open while Dad grabbed the barbed spears with pliers. The quills were stuck into the roof of Alex's mouth and in his tongue. Every quill left a few drops of blood where it had been embedded. Before long, Alex's mouth was raw. The whole job took over an hour; his cries lingered in the air for days. Fortunately, Alex recovered, though he seemed to hesitate before charging small animals.

As bad as the impaling stick, the skunks, and the porcupine quills were, Alex still had one great adventure left in his illustrious dog's life. It happened one day as we were climbing a mountain with some cousins who were visiting. We were up near the tree line, walking along a cliff ledge when I accidentally kicked a rock. Alex, who always chased anything I threw and knew no restraint, saw the rock spin out from under my foot and took off after it. To my horror, the rock tumbled off the cliff edge and into thin air. I shouted "No!" but Alex never slowed. He leaped from the cliff with nothing but empty space between his furry body and the conifer forest 100 yards below. Finding no traction in free-fall, he kicked and howled before disappearing

Hope for Nerds

into the trees below. We heard snapping branches, then only silence.

In blind panic, we ran the long hike around the cliff to the bottom where Alex landed. After two hours of fruitless searching, it grew dark, so we reluctantly gave up and hiked back down the mountain where our parents were waiting. I climbed into the van, someone asked where Alex was, and I broke down sobbing. I hated crying in front of my cousins—it was such a baby thing to do. But I'd lost my best friend, and nothing could replace him.

As a last-ditch hope, we posted a lost-dog advertisement on a local radio call-in program. I ran home every day after school asking Mom if anybody had called, but nobody had. I figured somebody might at least find his body so I could bury him out back.

Then one day someone did call, and sure enough, they had found Alex alive. They said he was in pretty good shape for having taken his first flying lesson, and they were surprised how much he ate. I didn't believe it was really Alex until I heard his bark over the phone. Right away Mom drove me to pick him up. Alex was so happy to see me that he cried... at least, I think those were his tears.

Chapter Seven
Battle of Wounded Cheek

Aside from Alex and I, several other neighborhood boys enjoyed the dairy land behind our house. One of them was a big, rough kid named Brad. He and I were never good friends—I didn't trust him—but once in a while I came across him playing along the creek, and I tried to get along with him anyway. Brad's parents were divorced, and he lived with his mother in the trailer court adjacent to our property, the same court where I had chased the wounded skunk. Back in those days there weren't many divorces, and you were supposed to feel sorry for a kid if his parents split up, so I tried. But one day, Brad's mother bought him the nicest, most expensive bike anyone had ever seen, so I stopped feeling sorry for him. Besides, Brad used to push all the neighborhood kids around. He was a lot bigger than me. Of course, everybody was a lot bigger than me.

Besides being a bully, Brad was amazingly deadly with a rock. He could hurl one with lethal accuracy like a national league pitcher. Once I saw him hit a goose flying at full speed along the creek. The rock smacked the goose's head, knocking it out and dropping it into the water. We pulled the goose ashore and examined it for several minutes, marveling at the wing span and sharp webbed feet. Suddenly it sprang to life, thrashing and snapping as we struggled to escape. Mercifully, it flew away, but not before inflicting a bevy of red welts on our skin.

I also saw Brad drop a flying duck with a rock. That one didn't recover. I heard he took it home and ate it. You never wanted to get on Brad's bad side. At least, not when he was angry.

Skinny Charley was one of my best friends, a nerd with big ideas like me. We liked to plan things and then build them together. During one long, hot summer when the creek was low and ambitions were high, we decided to build a fort extending from the creek bank to halfway over the water. It required careful planning and copious building materials. It took us several weeks to gather all of the wood from backyard junk piles and trash bins. We worked hard that summer and into the fall, sinking posts into the mucky creek bottom and then building a platform for the walls and roof. Eventually we had the best fort in the neighborhood. Everybody knew it, even Brad.

One day in early winter, Skinny Charley and I sat in our fort fooling around with our BB guns, telling stories, and making plans for a better fort. This time of year, the creek was high, surrounding our fort with freezing cold water, but we liked it that way. We extended a plank from the bank to access the fort without getting wet. Then we'd pull the plank into the fort so no one else could reach us. We felt safe in there, like knights in a castle surrounded by a mote. Nothing could touch us. We'd planned for everything. Almost.

Brad must have been watching us for a while, because when he launched his sneak attack, it was from our weakest

Battle of Wounded Cheek

front: the sky. Since none of the neighborhood kids could fly, we didn't give the roof much thought. But Brad did. The-rock-throwing-killer made a huge snowball and climbed up the big tree that hung out over the creek high above our fort. He planned on heaving the snowball down into a hole in the roof, blasting us with icy cold snow. But as Brad was getting ready to bomb us, Charley looked up and saw him. Grabbing his freshly loaded BB gun, Charlie yelled "Brad, you get out of here or I'll shoot."

Brad just laughed, so Charley shot him. That's when all hell broke loose. Brad cursed and grabbed his butt, jerking in pain so bad he lost his balance and came crashing through the tree branches and into the frigid water. SPLASH! It was a great shot and would have gone viral if YouTube had existed back then. But Brad wasn't about to be made a fool of by a couple of nerdy little kids. He stomped out of the creek, his enormous frame dripping with cold vengeance, yelling curses at Charley, me, the fort, the creek, nerds, and every winged creature that had ever crossed his sight.

We knew this was far from over. While the fort afforded some protection, we didn't want Brad to trap us, so we grabbed our BB guns and slithered across the plank, positioning ourselves on solid ground and waiting for the culmination of Brad's fury. Seeing us on dry land, Brad charged Skinny Charlie and ripped the BB gun from his hands, tossing it aside like a stick. Since I was the smallest, he probably didn't give me a second thought. Besides, I hadn't shot him. Charley had his tough face on, but I knew he was scared because he was just a skinny kid that anyone could whip. Brad grabbed Charley by the shirt and was readying to fist him. That's when I pressed my BB

Hope for Nerds

gun into Brad's face and said, "Brad, if you hit Charley, I'll shoot you."

Now, this was the second time that day Brad received such an invitation, and the first time must have left a sizable impression on him, because he froze. He didn't swing, and he didn't step back. It was a standoff from an old Western movie; all we needed was the high lonesome music. And as the seconds ticked off the minutes, nobody moved a muscle. I had the only gun, and it was pressed against Brad's flush face.

I don't know if I would have pulled the trigger in that moment, but neither did Brad. All I knew was that I had to stand up for Skinny Charley, my friend, my nerd friend.

Maybe it was staring down the barrel of my gun, maybe it was the stinging welt on his hind end, or maybe it was his dripping wet jacket forming ice crystals, but Brad finally turned and stomped off, reciting his colorful threats of vengeance on all things living or dead.

Brad made a good decision that day. He went on to stone many a flying fowl, but he always left us alone after that. Charlie and I planned our next fort, this time with a better roof. We also had a few good laughs over the Battle of Wounded Cheek, but never within earshot of Brad.

Chapter Eight
Those Skinny-Dipping Girls

While all the neighborhood boys spent time at the creek that ran behind our land, I spent more time there than anyone. I loved it. My dog Alex loved it, too. Of course, he loved anything I did. It was the freedom of isolation that attracted us. Alex and I could do whatever we wanted. No older brothers or sisters to tell us we couldn't. No parents to please. No rules to follow. Nothing but our own agenda.

As a card-carrying, board-certified nerd, I was pretty awkward around adults and girls my age. As a 13-year-old, I wasn't completely anti-social, just not well skilled in socializing. I didn't know how to talk with most people, so I never got any practice and never got any better. Every now and then a group of boys would show up at the creek bank, and we would swap stories about boy things: hunting, dogs, school, machines, and girls.

Skinny Charley—my best friend and fellow nerd who built the fort with me—used to tell stories that everyone knew were not true. Today, I'm sure he is an inventor or a politician or a bestselling author somewhere. With his creative flare, it was hilarious to hear him trying to convince us that his tall tales had even a shred of credibility. One day he told us how he built an airplane and flew it all over the state before it crashed. When we asked how he survived, he claimed to have escaped by holding on to the corners of his jacket and floating to the ground like a parachute. He was quick; I'll give him that. That's probably why I liked him: He knew how to dream.

When it came my turn, I told stories of the things Alex and I did—killing gophers and getting attacked by porcupines. After a while, our stories took on a life of their own, growing more alive with every telling. One of our favorite subjects was how fun it would be to show up at the creek and find a bunch of girls skinny-dipping. We even formulated a plan of action for this blessed event, agreeing to stay quiet and peep from the bushes, never letting the girls know we were there. Then we'd sneak up, take their clothes, and hide them. When the girls tried to get out and saw their clothes were gone, we would tease them for a while, hollering from the bushes and scaring them. We wouldn't give their clothes back until they screamed. Then we would be nice, because we still wanted them to like us. Maybe one of them would even give us a kiss for being so kind. Such was the courtship dreams of the prepubescent boys' group.

It could have worked. But it never happened because girls never came to the creek, let alone skinny dipped in it. Besides the water was dirty. But the story became more believable as we spun it over and over, refining every aspect of our plan.

One summer day, Skinny Charley and I each built rafts out of old logs we found along the bank. We tied them together with stout twine and wire—whatever we could salvage from our parents' garages. Since I had a crush on

Those Skinny-Dipping Girls

Karen—a pretty girl at school—I named my raft after her. Of course, I never told her; I don't think I even told Charlie. But I kept that raft for a whole year and often floated it out into the calm portions of the creek. Many an hour I drifted peacefully as I lay back and stared into the azure sky, dreaming of my bright future and pretty Karen.

Sometime after that year, I loaded my raft down with rocks and sank it to the bottom of the creek. Funny how life turns out. I never got the courage to speak to Karen, and I never did see those skinny-dipping girls.

Chapter Nine
Every Nerd Needs a Chemistry Set

My two brothers and I had our bedroom in the basement, but they grew up and moved out, leaving me the whole basement to myself—finally. The floor and walls were concrete, so it always felt damp and musty. The ceiling was the exposed joists of the floor above. The joists creaked and dust trickled down when people walked overhead. I hung old bed sheets over part of it to catch the dirt. It was perfect.

At the entrance to my bedroom, I had two swinging doors like an old saloon. When people walked into my bedroom, they knew they were entering a cool pad. Sure, few people ever came down there—nerds don't get many visitors—but that was all right with me. I had plenty to entertain myself, maybe even too much.

My favorite was my chemistry set. I inherited most of it from my two brothers, but I also got my hands on chemicals I probably shouldn't have had. Sure, I had the usual things like sulfur, sodium carbonate, and boric acid, but I also had saltpeter, which is a key ingredient to gunpowder. Yeah, man! I was a dangerous little nerd. And the best part was that my mother never knew. (Well…now she does. Sorry, Mom.)

Hope for Nerds

Things got a bit more interesting with the acquisition of chemicals from Mr. Burns, my science teacher. At the end of my freshman year, our Catholic school closed due to financial problems, and Mr. Burns gave me the leftover chemicals from the chemistry lab. I was one of his favorite students, and I guess he felt he could trust me. But Mr. Burns didn't let me have the bottle of potassium. Instead, I stayed after school one day and we had some fun with it. We threw it in a bucket of water to see what would happen. It was a good thing we were outside. It blew out a nice hole in the metal bucket and left a crater in the sidewalk that is probably there to this day.

Although he should have known better, Mr. Burns also gave me some unlabeled bottles that had been forgotten in the back closet since the Truman presidency. I had no idea what would happen when I mixed and heated these in my test tubes. It was fun finding out though. I got a lot of pops, bangs, and colorful flames in my basement laboratory. Fortunately, none ignited the wooden joists holding the house up above my head, so I considered my experiments a success. I also had fun heating a mixture of glycerin and sulphur, which made huge smoke clouds that quickly filled the whole basement. We didn't have smoke detectors in those days—probably a good thing, I guess.

Of course, not everything went so well; otherwise, I wouldn't be sharing this story.

One day my oldest brother Jim came home for a visit. He recommended a mixture of chemicals that he assured me do amazing things when heated together. I found out later that the mixture makes vapors that causes anyone nearby to vomit.

Every Nerd Needs a Chemistry Set

One night I was up late messing around with my potions when, on a whim, I poured some alcohol in a pan with a few other chemicals that I've forgotten. I held a lit match to the pan and FOOM! Brilliant orange and blue flames engulfed the pan and continued burning fiercely. With no lid and no fire extinguisher, I knew I was in trouble; I just didn't know how bad. Without a second thought, I heaved my panicked breath into the heart of the flames. The resulting flare up blew me backwards, enveloping my face in searing heat and darkness. After that huge flare up, the fire collapsed and then instantly went out.

My first thought was for my vision, which improved markedly when I opened my eyes. Then came the smell of burning hair and flesh. It took me a moment to realize whose hair and flesh. At least I wasn't smelling burning wood, so no need to alert my parents who were safely in bed, out of harm's way.

As my shock receded, so did the adrenaline rush. That's when the real pain started. The burning sensation on my skin meant it had to be bad. I rushed to a nearby mirror to inspect the damage. Terrified by now, I realized my whole face was red and my eyebrows were gone. My bangs, which were pretty important in those days—even to a nerdy chemist—had burned up, leaving little melt balls at the stub ends of every hair. Worst of all, however, was my nose. The top layer of skin was gone and bubbles appeared through the moist red flesh. It was a ghastly sight. I found a jar of Vaseline, smeared it all over my face in hope of instant improvement, and immediately regretted the decision. The skin screamed under my slight touch, but the more I stared at my reflection, the worse it got. Muttering to myself in the vernacular of the day, I said, "Harold, you're toast." Then the absurdity of my statement hit me, and I laughed giddily until the fear returned.

What would I tell my parents? And what would the kids at school think? I was never good at lying or making up lame excuses, but the repercussions of my actions reverberated through my overheated mind. What if Mom took my chemistry set? What if they made me sleep upstairs? What if I lost all my cool stuff and had to spend the rest of my days under their watchful gaze? This was worse than my melted bangs. This was a life of potent solitude. My nerd-dom was in peril.

I spent the night on my back—the only position tolerable—and hoped for a miraculous recovery by morning. It never came. Instead, I was beginning to appreciate the fact that I didn't burn the house down, which counted as the greatest miracle of the night. At breakfast, I just froze when my mother asked me what happened. When I finally said I didn't know, I could tell she wasn't buying it. Then Dad stepped in and bailed me out, saying I must have accidentally rubbed some chemical on my face. Dad was great; he understood my reticence. He probably sensed I'd done something stupid and didn't want to talk about it. He never got upset at things like that. As soon as he offered his explanation, the discussion was over and no one asked any more questions—at least not at home.

School was a different matter. Kids don't have to ask questions; they develop their own theories to enjoy your predicament. I got called Rudolf for a while, and then Mister Clean. One kid must have guessed right because he called me The Nutty Professor. But that was okay. I deserved all of it. Blowing on a flaming pan of chemicals? What was I thinking?

Chapter Ten
The Real Push-up Champion

In all my years going to school, I received one bad grade. It was a C- in religion class. Go figure. I kept trying to correct the priest who taught the class. He just wouldn't listen even though I patiently tried to help him understand how he should teach his class.

I was arrogant concerning ideas about God and religion. It became a lifelong problem. I simply thought I knew the truth on the related subjects. Of course, confidence is necessary for anyone to think independently of others' opinions, but that confidence welled into arrogance on a regular basis—especially later in life, when I attended seminary and tried to correct several professors on issues that they simply did not understand. Most of them were idiots and wouldn't listen to reason. Do you seen now what I was telling you about my problem with arrogance?

After my freshman year in high school, I transferred to a public school. As I mentioned earlier, the Catholic high school closed. Merging with thousands of non-Catholic students was an overwhelming transition, made worse by the fact that I was still the smallest kid around. If anything, I was even smaller now, as these non-Catholic kids seemed especially huge. Maybe it was the meat they ate on Fridays. Fortunately, events transpired that introduced me to the school in a grand way.

The first day of school was orientation day, when all the students visited the various school departments and chose their electives for the year. In the Athletic Department, the head coach held an exercise competition in the gymnasium for any guys interested in joining a sports team. The rest of the students—many of them, girls—were free to wander in, observe, and cheer or jeer their favorite competitors. Most of the guys competing were obviously school athletes—jocks with arms bigger than my legs. I scanned the field but didn't see any nerds out there, so I figured the safest place for me was on the bleachers with the rest of the cheering section. After a while I got bored, so I wandered about the gym floor, stepping around the human machines doing their jumping jacks, leg lifts, and arm rolls. They were doing their best to impress the coach and their future dates. It was marvelous to see what real muscles could do.

Toward the end of the period came the most important event: a pushup competition. About 70 guys each staked out an area on the gym floor, being sure to catch the eye of the particular girl they wanted to impress. Then the coach blew the whistle and the heaving began. To my surprise, I saw a friend out there, so I moved closer to cheer him on. The competition was fierce; most of the athletes were getting up around 100 pushups before quitting. Typically, the boys would hit their limit, and roll over on their backs, vapor rising from their spent chests. But my friend was still going strong, so I squatted down close to encourage him. With every pushup that he grunted out, I grunted with him. As he struggled, I got closer still, urging him

The Real Push-up Champion

on, matching my breathing with his. When he reached 130 push-ups and started to slow, I dropped to the floor and started doing pushups alongside him, driving him on.

As more and more guys dropped out, the students gathered around the strongest competitors, voicing their predictions for a victor. Soon, it was down to five or six boys. Oblivious to the rest of the gym floor, I kept doing pushups with my friend, calling out a cadence for both of us: "One-forty-one, one-forty-two, one-forty..." By then, a small crowd had gathered around us, including several pretty girls.

Finally my friend gave up, rolled onto his back and heaved a mighty sigh, but I kept going, caught up in the moment. Suddenly I was aware of cheering and realized that it was for me. Didn't they know I was only there to encourage my friend? Then it dawned on me: No one knew I had started doing push-ups at 130.

Well...with everyone yelling, I couldn't just quit and let them down. I was doing more push-ups than I ever dreamed possible, even if I did get a late start. Finally, the only other guy in the gym quit—a big, muscular jock with a single eyebrow across his forehead—and I was the last man left pushing. The place went wild. The little nerd was the pushup champion! I didn't know whether to be elated or ashamed. Actually, I was kind of confused.

No one except my friend knew I hadn't really won, but he wasn't going to tell anyone, and the crowds were so excited I couldn't have convinced them anyway. So I let them crown me the push-up champion of the school. It was a great way to start a new school, especially as the smallest kid in the place.

With my new found fame, I did something outrageous about two months later. All of the guys were in the locker room dressing out for gym class when the football quarterback came up to me and tested me with a stupid remark. I don't know what got into me, but I rose up into his face and repeated words that my brother Jim once said to me: "I am about to stuff your puny ass under that closet and you will soon be looking out at the world crying like a baby!" I said it quietly. I said it like Jim would have said it. The whole locker room fell silent. He was three times my size, the most-loved champion of the school, with the prettiest girls screaming to bear his children. I had two nerd friends looking at me with terror on their faces, but I didn't flinch.

Testosterone flooded the room. It came from everyone except the nerds because our voices had not yet changed. A long period of silence passed, but that jock couldn't think of anything to say. He was dumbfounded. He slouched his posture and then smiled at me. We were friends from that day forward.

To make that school year even better, I had a run-in with Brad—yeah, the same Brad skinny Charley had shot with his BB gun two years earlier. Brad was going to the same high school, but he was a basketball jock. Needless to say, I wasn't.

One day I was walking down the school hallway during the lunch break. I walked by the area where the jocks hung out, and Brad jumped out of their ripped-muscle brotherhood and yelled at me. He had a plastic cup with Seven-up in one hand, which was a good thing, because he

The Real Push-up Champion

took a swing at me with his other hand, and as he did the Seven-up went splashing across the tile floor. Brad missed me by a long shot, and as I pulled away, he jumped at me again, but this time his foot slipped on the Seven-up he had spilled. Swoosh, his legs flew out from under him, and he was flat on this back unable to move. All the jocks were watching and started laughing. I just kept walking along and, even though I had never touched Brad, somehow the incident grew into an anecdote about why everyone better stay away from the push-up champion. It helped a lot that the football quarterback liked me.

I have always felt supernaturally protected. It started way back then. It has made me fearless in many difficult places around the world.

Chapter Eleven
The Night I Broke Dad's Heart

In the late 1960s, the world seemed to be in turmoil. Forces were pulling society apart, forcing it to change in ways unthinkable a decade before. My family was a microcosm of that turbulence. My brother Jim was in college training to be a Catholic priest, while Claude was headed to Thailand as a soldier supporting the Vietnam War—a conflict that most Americans vehemently opposed. Fern, the perfect sister, started college and inexplicably pulled away from family relationships. My other sisters, Patsy and Rose, remained at home with me, all of us trying to figure out life for ourselves. That was the mantra of our age—find yourself.

Patsy and Rose had bedrooms upstairs, while I reigned over the basement. Patsy would leave her gum stuck to the wall at the bottom of the staircase so she could pick it off and chew it later. More than once I replaced that wad of gum with some I had chewed, but I never told her (until now). Rose was quiet and thoughtful, but the boys at school thought she was cute.

One evening Patsy experimented with an Ouija board. Some of her friends had had weird experiences with theirs. When Patsy brought a board home, the whole house got spooky. It was hard to define, but I struggled to sleep at

Hope for Nerds

night. I kept sensing dark figures in the corners of my room. Patsy must have felt it too, because she finally got rid of the board. I was glad to see it go.

Sometimes Patsy and Rose went out at night and "cruised the drag," the main activity for restless teenagers in our town. Anyone with a car and some gas (only 17 cents per gallon back then) would slowly drive up and down Main Street on Friday and Saturday nights, honking at other kids, connecting with friends, and generally strutting their stuff. Once I got into high school, my sisters let me tag along a few times; it was enough to give me the feel for cruising, which to my nerd sensibilities seemed rather pointless. One night, Rose talked an older boy into buying some vodka for us, and we all shared it. That was my first attempt at getting drunk. I got sick to my stomach quickly and didn't even get dizzy. It was my last attempt at getting drunk.

Perhaps it was my age or the rampant social upheaval of our day, but I grew hungry for spiritual truth. Seeking answers beyond our family's deeply-held religious values, I took the family Bible prominently displayed on a table in our living room and began reading it in my basement bedroom every night. To my surprise, I found words there that contradicted things I'd always been taught. Soon, I began questioning all my family's Catholic beliefs.

If I had been raised in a different era, I probably would not have challenged so deeply, but these were days of societal revolution. Teenagers were being encouraged to reject the beliefs of their parents. The phrase generation gap had been coined by the media to describe the gap of understanding emerging between young people and adults. A

The Night I Broke Dad's Heart

popular expression at the time was: "Never trust anyone over 30." Youth were led to believe they were smarter and more advanced than their parents and modern science was advancing so quickly that elders simply couldn't keep up. Talk of the generation gap was on television every day, feeding the alienation between young and old. The media was actually creating the generation gap by their constant reporting of it. Back then, it effectively fueled a generation of isolated skeptics.

My questioning of religious beliefs came to a head one day during the Easter season when my brothers and sisters were home for a visit. Mom and Dad wanted everyone to go to evening Mass together. After Mass, we were expected to attend confession. Now, for those who don't understand Catholic practices, confession is the sacrament when a person confesses all of his or her sins to a priest in a small, dark room, separated by a screen. The priest listens and then gives absolution, which is his blessing and decree that your sins are forgiven. Catholics take great stock in this practice, for it means they are right with God after saying a prayer or two.

That evening after Mass, each of my siblings dutifully went into the confessional booth and came out absolved of their sins, but when my turn came, I refused to go. Dad gave me a stern look, but I didn't budge. I had never defied my father before. Suddenly, I was on dangerous territory. Since he could not discipline me at church without making a scene, I had some time, but I knew this only delayed the inevitable. An uneasy silence fell over our family as we packed into the van and drove home together. Not a word was spoken, but every person in that van understood that the baby of the family was in deep trouble.

After pulling into our garage, Dad told everyone else to go into the house. Then he turned to me with the same look I'd seen in church. For the first time in my life, I was afraid he might beat me. But he didn't. Instead, he just pointed to the back pasture and said, "Run!"

He had me run a long time that night. Through the dim light of flickering stars, he watched me from the backyard. I could feel his eyes as I struggled to avoid the grass clumps, sticks, and holes that could easily turn an ankle or break a leg.

While I was running, I couldn't help but think his frustration with me was more than my challenge of our Catholic faith. In the preceding few months I had been pretty sedentary, watching television every evening. He had made several comments to me about it, but I had shrugged it off. Running the length of that field over and over again, I felt like a terrible disappointment to him.

Finally, he called me in and sent me to bed, and that was it. He never said any more about the issue. I knew there was nothing to discuss, but at the time, I did not know why. Today, as a parent myself, I understand what it feels like to see your children grow up and assume independence before you are ready for their emancipation—to have them challenge everything you hold sacred; to depart from your protection and faint light, facing dangers you know could easily destroy them. Back then, I only knew I had upset Dad. Today I know I broke his heart.

As is the way of healthy families, there must have been some eventual healing, for in the years that I remained at home, Dad changed toward me. Once my brothers and

The Night I Broke Dad's Heart

sisters were mostly grown and on their own, Dad seemed to have more time for me. He took me fishing several times. At first, I thought he was just letting me tag along, but sometimes he wouldn't even fish. He'd just sit along the stream watching the water flow by as I caught my limit. Other times, he seemed content to hang around me, making small talk and enjoying my company. In previous years, he never seemed to have time to do that with any of us. Something changed when he got older. I guess being the baby of the family had its advantages; perhaps he wanted to hang on to his last child as the empty nest years approached.

As I matured, Dad never could accept my departure from the Catholic faith. If I happened to bring up any subject relating to religion, he would stand up and leave the room or walk away. When I visited my parents, I would attend the Catholic Mass with them, and though I didn't walk forward for communion or go to confession, I continued to sense the presence of God while sitting in the pew.

Dad and Mom never stopped praying that my siblings and I would return to the Catholic Church, Jim was the only one who remained committed to the practices of our religious upbringing. Although he tried, Jim never became a priest. A pretty lady snared his heart which led to marriage, settling down, and raising a family.

Jim has since passed away of a rare disease, and Mom lives with Linda (my wife) and me, along with my sister Rose, who helps care for Mom. Dad is a resident in a nearby facility that cares for patients with Alzheimer's. Medications keep Dad going, and they also keep a smile on his face. Although he no longer recognizes me when I visit, I no longer see in his eyes disappointment caused by his son's decision to leave the Catholic faith.

Chapter Twelve
Escaping into the Wilds

As I grew into my teenage years, hunting became very important to me. I loved animals—still do—and I enjoyed taking them from the wilderness as much as I enjoyed the company of live animals. My adventures in the mountains, however, came as much from an awkwardness with people as a love of the wild. I just couldn't seem to relate to my fellow humans, and after a while, I gave up.

My stalwart companion as I headed into the wild was a '59 Ford pickup truck, affectionately named "Ol' Yeller." (Can you guess what color she was?) I'd purchased her for $125, and she never let me down. Ol' Yeller and I shared many an adventure trekking across mountain roads that would have scared a goat.

During the winter I trapped a lot of foxes, coyotes, and bobcats. Being raised in the country, I had little compassion for predators. I killed as many as possible. Of course, those were different times; people's values have changed dramatically since then, and so have mine.

Yet, very little went to waste from the animals I killed. I always made good use of the furs. I sold most of them for a tidy profit, but I also learned how to tan furs, preserving their beauty. This skill developed into my hobby of taxidermy. I eventually set up a shop in our basement next to my chemistry set. The area was soon filled with critters mounted for display. I had everything there, even a few skunks—the trickiest of animals to skin because of the notorious bags of acid located under the tail.

It's not a good idea to skin a skunk in the house. One wrong move and the rancid smell of skunk vengeance hangs in the air for weeks. Once I tried to save the juice in a plastic container. I found out the hard way that skunk juice is such a strong acid that it eats through plastic. I wondered how it didn't eat through the skunk's flesh.

Mom had a six-foot-long freezer in the basement that I gradually took over with my animal carcasses. Whenever I had time, I thawed a critter out and set to work. Everything I needed was in my basement laboratory. Sometimes the smells from my work would rise upstairs and gross my sisters out. I considered that a win-win situation. My basement looked like a still-life zoo—a wildlife museum suspended in time.

As my taxidermy improved, I advertised my skills in a local newspaper. That's when I learned a bit about business and a lot about the blessings of God.

A classmate had shot a hawk (illegal today) and wanted me to mount it. Eager to show off my skills, I brought the hawk home and promptly skinned it, but I made a stupid mistake that ruined the skin and destroyed any chance of mounting my classmate's trophy. I was devastated, certain my reputation as a taxidermist would be shattered. All I could do was hang my head and regret I'd ever tried.

Later that day, as I sat on the porch sulking, something amazing happened. Let me assure you: Everything you are about to read is the truth and nothing but the truth, so help me. A hawk flew out of the sky and into our garage through the opened door. I stared into the garage, completely amazed to see this hawk, nearly identical to the one I had just ruined, perched on the workbench.

It took a bit for my brain to believe my eyes, but as soon as I could think clearly, I rushed into the house and grabbed my pellet gun. I ran back toward the garage and slowed my steps as I approached, attempting to calm my racing heart. I peeked my head around the corner into the garage. In the time it had taken me to get my gun, the hawk hadn't moved. I'd never known a hawk to behave this way. It was just sitting there waiting for me to shoot it! So, not wanting to disappoint the creature, I took careful aim, let out my breath, and dropped the bird right where it stood.

To this day, I do not know if that hawk's appearance was simply the result of God intervening in the natural order of things to show His love for me, or if that hawk coming to me was the natural outworking of the dominion God gave humanity over the animals. Whatever, it solved my dilemma.

On numerous occasions I have observed wild animals seeming to act totally counter to their natural instinct for survival. For example, one morning I was sighting in my gun before going coyote hunting. I focused on a stump far off on a mountainside, and as I prepared to shoot, a coyote ran up and stopped right in front of the very stump on which I was focused. I never saw that coyote until he appeared in the cross hairs of my scope. It was as if he was obediently offering himself to me. I decided, however, to let him walk away.

Another similar incident occurred one day when I went hunting with a friend who, for some unexplained reason, had an uncommon authority with wolves. Sure enough, we got out of my pickup that day and three wolves ran out of the woods and stood directly in front of us—not more than 30 feet away. The alpha wolf stood motionless looking us in the eyes as if waiting for our instructions.

I had observed this behavior with other animals as well. People untrained and unfamiliar in the ways of the wild may never experience this, but there is a connection between the hunter and the hunted that cannot be explained in biological terms.

On the day the hawk flew into my garage I was given another chance, a redemptive do-over if you will. I had ruined my friend's bird, but another showed up to offer himself. Wasting no time, I prepared the sacrificial hawk and mounted it in place of the one I had ruined. When I presented the trophy to my friend, he was delighted.

I've waited a long time to share this story in public. I guess I'm safe now. (What's the statute of limitations on hawk-swapping, anyway?) When I think about that wild hawk suddenly gliding into our garage, I shake my head in wonder.

Throughout my high school years, as my passion for

hunting grew, I dreamed of owning a cabin in Alaska where I could get away from people. I was certain life in the wild with a good dog would be the most wonderful existence any man could know. I figured that in total isolation my anxiety of being around people would be eliminated. I didn't like people. Or maybe I did. Perhaps I just didn't like myself when I was around them. Yeah, that's it. I just didn't like how awkward and inferior I felt around others.

But that was all going to change.

Chapter Thirteen
Living on Highway Pizza

Despite all the denouncements from my loving, caring older siblings regarding my intellectual prowess, I managed to finish high school at 17. Before going to college, I decided to take a year off and follow a dream I'd had for a while: driving across the country for the summer.

I didn't have much money, but that was OK. I had a plan. On the back of Ol' Yeller—my '59 Ford pickup—I built a cabin out of some used lumber I had salvaged. I nailed the rude boards together into a tight box that fit snugly over the pickup bed. It was big enough for a propane stove, my bed, and plenty of supplies. It would be my home while I traveled around America.

Being made from raw lumber, my cabin needed a paint job, but I didn't have enough of any one color to cover it, so I mixed several cans together and painted my new home with a roller. It takes a long time for paint to dry when it is a mixture of latex and oil-based colors.

The finished product didn't look so great but many blemishes were covered over. While I can't prove this, I'm sure it also filled in a few of the air leaks from where the boards didn't seal so well. Beaming with pride, I admired my handiwork until Dad saw it and announced with a big

Hope for Nerds

smile on his face that it looked like puke. He was right, I guess. But it was my home—puke on the outside, cozy on the inside.

With my preparations complete, the joyous day came when I eagerly loaded Ol' Yeller with a warm sleeping bag, a little bit of food, a rifle, and my taxidermy tools. I said good-bye to my parents, tried not to look back as they waved, and drove away. Mom was probably crying. I suspect Dad was smiling. I won't tell you how I felt. This was Montana; big boys didn't have feelings back then.

I drove high into the mountains to a place I had previously visited but had dreamed of experiencing again. It was a stunningly beautiful place with canyon walls reaching to the clouds and coyotes howling every night. And there were plenty of squirrels which I shot, then turned into jerky in preparation for the days ahead.

I felt deeply at peace and I never spoke to a single person—my idea of perfection. To my great surprise, however, I grew extremely lonely after about two weeks. This wasn't in my plan at all. So to keep myself company, I kept a diary and found myself writing about how meaningless life is without people. Was this me—Harold the Nerd—pining for human company? As idyllic as those weeks were, I decided that living alone was not the utopia I'd anticipated. Encouraged by this revelation, I resolved to return to civilization and embrace a different kind of isolation—that of being alone in the midst of civilization.

Emerging from my remote mountain fortress, I started traveling around the Northwest USA. I stuck mainly to back roads and small towns, drinking coffee in greasy diners, listening to locals, learning about the area, and looking for dead animals along the road.

Those carcasses were pure gold to me. When I came across road kill, I stopped and looked it over. If it didn't smell too bad, and if it seemed in good enough shape for mounting, I took it into my camper and went to work with my taxidermy tools.

As my skills for spotting dead animals sharpened, I shifted gears and started looking for live ones, too. If a critter crossed the road in front of me, I'd try to hit it. My aim got pretty good after a while, but hunting with a pickup truck was also a dangerous (OK—stupid) way to hunt. I actually ran off the road a couple of times and found myself stuck in a muddy ditch, proving that nature evens the odds between the hunter and the hunted. I'm sure there were a few gophers and rabbits that escaped my squealing bald tires, laughing and telling their friends about the nerd they left stuck in the mud.

Road hunting also had long-term negative consequences in my life. I was constantly scanning the landscape for animals, and every time I spotted one I would get a rush of adrenaline. Seeing animals became *really* important to me. So much so that 20 years later I could not drive across the country without obsessively searching for anything with fur or feathers. I saw a lot of game, but I also found myself unable to relax and watch the road. Like an alcoholic looking for his next drink, I was desperate to see critters. With such intensity, I would be exhausted after any long drive. I didn't realize what a problem it was until I was about 40 years old, unable to think about anything but roaming animals while I drove. So then I prayed for God to help me and forced myself to drive without looking around. This may be difficult for some readers to understand, but it took me almost a year of restraining myself before I felt free.

When I first learned to road hunt at 17 years old, I picked up a lot of animals. Parked at some campsite, I would remove and preserve the skin, then mount the animal to the best of ability hoping to make it look alive.

After a while, with a good number of animals mounted, I began parking at rest areas along the highway to sell my wares. On one side of my camper, I had built a large shelf that folded out to display the animals. I wasn't a very good salesman, but there wasn't a lot of competition for roadside taxidermy. I mean, how often do you see someone selling dead animals at a rest stop? People were curious and always came to see my work. They probably also wanted to meet the nut crazy enough to embark on this enterprise. The occasional sales I made gave me enough money for gas and basic supplies as I continued my trek across our great nation.

I rarely wasted anything from the animals I found or truck-hunted. In fact, the best part of my success was nourishment. On the back of my camper, I installed two long poles on hinges to stand them high into the air. A rope ran between the tops of the poles forming a clothesline for whatever laundry I had washed in a creek or rest-area sink.

When I wasn't drying clothes, I used the line for another purpose. From the wild animals that I had picked

Living on Highway Pizza

up, I cut the meat into thin strips, seasoned it with salt and other spices, and hung it across the clothesline suspended high into the air. With the wild meat swinging in the wind, it took about an hour of driving to turn it into jerky—my primary food on the road. Today, I can't imagine what it looked like to other motorists. Seems to me, I was occasionally the object of amazement to a station wagon full of vacationing kids, but I rarely took notice of people in those days. Perhaps somewhere in America, at this very moment, somebody is writing their memoirs of summer trips in the Northwest, and their fourth chapter starts with: "The strangest thing I ever saw while motoring across America with my family was this yellow truck with a puke-colored camper and…"

Of course, man does not live by jerky alone. So I fished when I could. When funds permitted, I'd treat myself to something I couldn't hit along the road, like a can of soup. I didn't always use my camper stove; fuel was precious. So to heat up my treasure, I'd wire the can onto the manifold of Ol' Yeller's engine. After 30 minutes of driving, the can was warm enough for eating. As good as that was, I sometimes broke down completely and splurged on a loaf of bread and jars of peanut butter and jelly. That was high living.

However, nothing could beat my favorite meal: fresh gopher. I know…I know…you'll just have to trust me on this; it is an acquired taste. I figure I have eaten more gophers than anyone alive. It's great on the open road. With a little sage, it tastes just like chicken.

You may think such living is crazy, but I figure God had me eating such foods to prepare my stomach for all of the unknown foods I would someday be eating in third-world countries on the mission field.

Anyway, it was a great summer. Very little went as planned, but I learned a lot. Ol' Yeller held together just fine and so did I. I highly recommend such an experience to anyone with even a wisp of wanderlust in their soul. Feel free to take my ideas. Of course, if too many people start doing this, there will be a serious shortage of gophers and a lot more taxidermy competition at the rest areas. Then the government will get involved and ruin it for everybody. So maybe we should franchise roadside taxidermy trucks now. This could be a whole new industry. One of my entrepreneurial readers could run with this idea. I wouldn't mind a bit. Of course, giving me a small cut off the top would be the right thing to do.

In return, I'll share my favorite gopher recipes.

Chapter Fourteen
Training to be a Wildlife Biologist

After my adventurous summer on the road, I returned to my parents' home and made plans for my future. Little did I know that God was also making plans.

My sister Rose, who was temporarily living at home, had been invited to a Bible study sponsored by a Baptist church—quite a departure from our Catholic upbringing. I went along with her, partly out of curiosity and partly out of spiritual hunger. We heard ideas that evening we had never been exposed to before. The Bible study leader explained how we could have a personal relationship with God and said we needed to be born again. The leader led Rose and me in a prayer for salvation, but I didn't understand what I was doing. Yet, something changed in me. I went home that night and began to realize how selfishly I was living. Lying in bed, I tossed and turned until early morning. Sure, I had not committed any serious sins ("mortal sins" in Catholic lingo), but I was suddenly and starkly aware of how I lived my life totally for my own pleasure, pursing my own desires with little regard for anyone else. I couldn't escape the conviction; it hung over me like a dirty blanket that I was desperate to shed.

Next week's Bible study couldn't come soon enough. I sat in the same room and heard a similar message, only this time it spoke clearly to my heart. At the end of the teaching, the leader invited us to pray. I prayed the same prayer, inviting Jesus into my life and accepting His forgiveness, but this time, I understood it, I meant it, and I wanted it.

Nothing changed, but everything changed. The conviction was gone—answered and forgiven. Love took its place. I was aware of a new life inside. Rose and I both shared an intoxicating joy. My sister-in-blood had become my sister in Christ.

Today as a look back, I believe the most significant change was that we made our faith our own. It was no longer the faith of our parents, but God revealed His love to us personally. That is what we accepted.

As newly-minted Christians, we immediately wanted to do something for God—spread the word, help people, lead others in the same prayer that infused us with such joy. So three weeks after Rose and I had given our lives to Jesus, we filled Ol' Yeller with gas, laid out a route, and headed to the nearest place we could think of with a healthy reputation for rampant sin: Las Vegas, Nevada. Surely we would find some people there who needed help.

At the end of the two days drive, we didn't know where to begin, so we stopped at a roadside church and asked to talk to a pastor. The pastor who met with us must have thought we were hippies looking for a hand-out because he didn't treat us very well. We told him we were new converts to Jesus and simply wanted to find somewhere that we could help people. Instead of welcoming our zeal, however, he called us "do-gooders" and urged us to move on. We were crestfallen, but we were also young, so we rebounded quickly. Rose and I even began to call each other "do-gooder," a sarcastic remark that still surfaces from time to time.

We ended up north of Las Vegas in a small farming community where migrant workers were harvesting vegetables. We joined them and spent hot summer days working the fields on our hands and knees. Most of the workers only spoke Spanish, so our communication was limited. Added to our difficulties was the fact that whenever we said "Jesus" a several of them would answer "Si?"

Having traveled so far from home, hoping to help real people with dire needs, I guess we expected spectacular results. But it seemed we merely ended up becoming part of their community without accomplishing anything significant.

At the end of that summer, having learned a little Spanish and a lot about vegetables, we traveled home to Montana and prepared for the next stage of life. Rose met a guy and settled down to raise a family. I enrolled in a university to begin training as a wildlife biologist.

At the university, I roomed on a dormitory floor where other wildlife students lived. We all had our interests in nature, and several of us remained active in the wild, especially on weekends. I trapped bobcats, foxes, and coyotes to pay college expenses. Some students hunted big game whenever possible, and others housed various animals in their dorm rooms even though it was forbidden. At one time our resident advisor had 17 live rattlesnakes in his

Hope for Nerds

room, while another student hung two elk from his ceiling. They were deceased, of course. Live elk would never have put up with such shenanigans.

A guy down the hall from me hit a jack rabbit on the highway one morning, and when he stopped to check it out, he discovered it was a female rabbit with 8 babies wiggling inside. So he did a C-section right there and then raised those bunnies in his dorm room. I brought home a bobcat one day—deceased—and the whole floor got together while we barbecued and ate it.

We really weren't breaking any dormitory rules by skinning dead animals in our rooms, because no one ever thought of making rules to forbid such things. Had there been rules, I would have been the worst offender, skinning everything from skunk to mountain lion in my dorm room. Needless to say, our floor had a different aroma than the rest of the campus, and so did we.

One evening I skinned a porcupine in my dorm room and by the time I finished I was too tired to carry the carcass out to the trash. So I wrapped it in a plastic garbage bag and threw it out my dorm window. That is not as bad as it sounds. Four floors down there was a courtyard completely enclosed and surrounded by dorm rooms. The courtyard was locked during the nights and no one could get inside. I just figured that I would get up early, retrieve the plastic bag with its contents, and toss it all into the campus garbage.

I overslept the next morning. When I did get out of bed, I immediately remembered the porcupine waiting in

Training to be a Wildlife Biologist

the courtyard so I hurried down to finish my job from the previous evening. To get to the courtyard, I had to take the stairs to the first floor, pass through the dorm lobby, and then down a hallway. When I entered the lobby, I saw a huge crowd of students. I quickly remembered that it was election day when students have the opportunity to vote for their favorite classmates to represent them before the powers that be at the university. A major voting station was set up in the lobby of our dormitory, so dozens of students were standing around waiting for their chance to vote.

Seeing the crowd I had second thoughts about retrieving that porcupine carcass, but Mom always taught me to clean up after myself. I slipped into the courtyard, grabbed the plastic bag, and began to walk down the hallway, trying to look as if nothing special was happening. But then I realized that blood was dripping from a hole in the bottom of the bag. I decided to run so as not to leave a thick blood trail. Then disaster hit. Just as I entered into the lobby, the bottom of the plastic bag ripped completely open. I had a enough speed and momentum to launch that carcass right into the middle of the crowd.

Sliding on its back, with its paws and feet sticking up, it looked a lot like a human baby soaked in blood. It was greasy enough to make it slide nicely on the hard tile surface. It left a solid streak of blood and fat tissue, then stopped almost in the very center of the lobby where it freaked everyone out.

So I did the only thing I knew to do. I acted as if nothing was unusual as I picked it up and slid it back into the bag. Everyone was silent. Nothing was said. I walked out with my baby-looking carcass and every thing went back to normal. However, after I disposed of the porcupine, I re-entered the dorm building through a back door so I wouldn't have to see anyone again.

There were several other such experiences, but none of them ever dampened my enthusiasm for working with wild animals. However, my adventures into the wilds took a major hit on New Year's Day of my freshman year.

I hiked deep into the mountains even though the temperatures hovered at a lethal minus 20 degrees F (not counting the wind chill factor). I'd left Ol' Yeller along the road and hiked five miles along a river that worked its way through an isolated canyon. The object of my quest was bobcat furs, which fetched a nice profit and kept me in college. Of course, to get the fur, I first had to get the bobcats, and that was what the traps were for. Knowing I didn't have much time in the severe cold kept me moving with a sense of urgency. It also caused me to forgo my usual caution.

As I trekked along my trap line, paying more attention to the surroundings than my footing, my right boot plunged through the thin ice of the river and became soaked up to my calf. I immediately realized the danger and figured my best chance of saving my foot lay with getting a fire started. Unfortunately, as a poor college student, I was not well prepared. I pulled my hands out of my gloves and fished for the meager supply of wooden matches stashed in my jacket. I managed to gather some dry kindling, but by now, my hands had frozen stiff and I could not hold a match in my fingers. In desperation, I tried to start the fire while holding the lit match between my teeth, but I only burnt my lips. After failing to start a fire, I decided my next best option was to hike out with my rapidly freezing leg, get back to Ol' Yeller, and find somebody who could help me.

At 20 below zero, no animals were moving except me. They stood still for their survival, but mine relied on my continual motion. Hiking out, I walked right through a herd of deer that didn't bother to move out of my way; they must have sensed I was in deep trouble and no threat to them. I finally caught up to Ol' Yeller, tears of agony frozen on my burnt cheeks. She fired up on the first try, and we made our way down the road with a leg gone dead below the ankle.

I reached the first house that I saw, limped to the door, and banged hard. Fortunately, this was Montana; one look at me was all the man needed to put away the gun, take me in, and start first aid. He phoned the nearest hospital, and a doctor told him how to treat me. Because the boot was frozen to my flesh, the doctor had him soak my foot in warm water before cutting the boot and my wool socks off in small pieces, carefully separating them from my skin. As my flesh revived, pain returned with a vengeance.

With the boot finally stripped off and my ashen gray foot wrapped in a blanket, I was driven to the emergency room that was two hours away. The doctor gave me some sobering news: To prevent the spread of gangrene, he'd have to cut off some or all of my foot. Now, a life of stomping around the mountains on a peg leg horrified me, and I begged him to give my foot a chance. "OK," he finally said, "Overnight, but if your circulation is not improved by morning, I will have to operate."

In the meantime, somebody had called my sister Patsy and a Christian friend at the university. Once word of my condition spread, my Christian friends organized a prayer vigil for which I will be forever grateful. In the morning, each of my toes had blood circulating through them, so the doctor relented. My battle wasn't over, though. I lost all of my toe nails on both feet and spent a month fighting a staph infection that swelled one leg into a balloon of bone and fluid. The muscles and nerves deteriorated to such an extent that it took a year for me to walk normally again without crutches or a pronounced limp. It turned out to be a year of reorienting my life in another direction.

Chapter Fifteen
God Changed this Nerd

After I returned to the university, my heart was being pulled farther from the wilds and propelled toward Christian ministry. A Christian leader began to disciple me on the fundamentals of Christianity—how to pray, how to share my faith, and how to teach God's word. As my desire to be engaged in full-time ministry grew, I knew I needed to overcome my crippling sense of inferiority and social ineptitude. I would never be able to reach people for Christ as a nerd. So in my fledgling faith, I prayed God would give me confidence and make me bold to reach others for Him.

Now, for the average person, this might be a casual request tossed up to heaven from the back roads of life. But for me, it was tantamount to Moses requesting passage for two million freaked-out Hebrews through the Red Sea. Still, the greater the need, the greater the zeal. Determined to change, I committed to praying every morning for God's help in transforming me from being a quiet, shy nerd to being comfortable around people. I wanted to accomplish something significant with my life, and I knew He would have to anoint me to do it. Even then, I was sensing that I wanted to change the world. To do so, God would first have to change me.

Hope for Nerds

On the 25th day of praying with this determined mind set, the presence of God enveloped me. I don't know any other way to describe it. God showed up. I knew it was God just as I knew my dad's voice or my mom's touch. Miraculously, I was filled with a new love for God and for people. I felt my heart change; I felt winds of the spirit blow into me and turn me. My orientation was forever altered in a God way, pointed toward His most precious creation: my fellow man.

I was still Harold, but I was a new Harold, a better Harold, the Harold God meant for me to be. I don't know how, when, or where I grew into such a nerd. Maybe it was being the youngest or the smallest or simply the cutest (definitely the cutest). But I changed that day, and everything in me rejoiced like a prisoner being released from a life sentence. This is who I always was but could never seem to be. This is who I longed for during those two weeks alone in my mountain paradise. This was every conversation I couldn't seem to pull off, every word I choked back, every drink of compassion I wanted to offer but instead watched slip through my fingers. This was the reservoir of love deposited in me, now released, which would propel me into ministry.

My experience was similar to 1 Samuel 10:6: "Then the Spirit of the Lord will come upon you mightily, and you shall...be changed into another man."

I was changed into a new man!

The change might not have seemed instantaneous to my friends, who still had to put up with my occasional nerdy ways, but for me it was dramatic. Something had occurred in my heart to place my life on a different path. Within a month, I became the student leader of Campus Crusade for Christ on our campus. I also met the girl of my dreams and eventually proposed. Linda became the wonderful woman to whom I have been married for over 36 years.

In the years that followed, I have had many experiences with God, each changing me in some significant way and redirecting my life. However, nothing has had the same impact as my transformation from a socially inept nerd to a leader and lover of people. When I think of the change God worked in me, I am filled with gratitude. During my youth, I was never involved in drugs, sex, or crime, but when I hear battle-scarred Christians share their remarkable testimonies of being delivered from abuse, gangs, or prison, I know they have not experienced any greater deliverance than I have.

Once I was a nerd, but now I'm free.

Other Books by Harold R. Eberle

Christianity Unshackled

Most Christians in the Western world have no idea how profoundly their beliefs have been influenced by their culture. What would Christianity be like if it was separated from Western thought? After untangling the Western traditions of the last 2,000 years of Church history, Harold R. Eberle offers a Christian worldview that is clear, concise, and liberating. This will shake you to the core and then leave you standing on a firm foundation!

Compassionate Capitalism:
A Judeo-Christian Value

As you read this book, you will learn how capitalism first developed as God worked among the Hebrew people in the Old Testament. The resulting economic principles then transformed Western society as they spread with Christianity. However, our present form of capitalism is different than that which God instilled in Hebrew society. What we need to do now is govern capitalism wisely and apply the principles of capitalism with compassion.

Releasing Kings for Ministry in the Marketplace
By John S. Garfield and Harold R. Eberle

"Kings" is what we call Christian leaders who have embraced the call of God upon their lives to work in the marketplace and from that position transform society. This book explains how marketplace ministry will operate in concert with local churches and pastors. It provides a Scriptural basis for the expansion of the Kingdom of God into all areas of society.

Other Books by Harold R. Eberle

Victorious Eschatology
Coauthored by
Harold R. Eberle and Martin Trench

Here it is—a biblically-based, optimistic view of the future. Along with a historical perspective, this book offers a clear understanding of Matthew 24, the book of Revelation, and other key passages about the events to precede the return of Jesus Christ. Satan is not going to take over this world. Jesus Christ is Lord and He will reign until every enemy is put under His feet!

Jesus Came Out of the Tomb... So Can You!
A Brief Explanation of
Resurrection-based Christianity

Forgiveness of sins is at the cross. Power over sin is in the resurrection and ascension. Yet, most Christians have no idea how to access the benefits of our Lord's resurrection and ascension. They are locked into death-centered Christianity, rather than life-centered Christianity. This book empowers the reader to make the transition and "come out of the tomb."

Grace...the Power to Reign
The Light Shining from Romans 5-8

We struggle against sin and yearn for God's highest. Yet, on a bad day it is as if we are fighting against gravity. Questions go unanswered:

- Where is the power to overcome temptations?
- Is God really willing and able to breathe into us so that our dry bones can live and we can stand strong?

For anyone who has ever struggled to live godly, here are the answers.

Other Books by Harold R. Eberle

Precious in His Sight
(Third edition)
A Fresh Look at the Nature of Humanity

How evil are we? How can I love myself if I am evil? What happened when Adam sinned? How does that sin influence us? Where do babies go when they die? This book has implication upon our understanding of sin, salvation, who God is, evangelism, and how we live the victorious Christian life.

Who Is God?

Challenging the traditional Western view of God, Harold R. Eberle presents God as a Covenant-maker, Lover, and Father. Depending on Scripture, God is shown to be in a vulnerable, open and cooperative relationship with His people. This book is both unsettling and enlightening—revolutionary to readers—considered by many to be Harold's most important contribution to the Body of Christ.

Developing a Prosperous Soul
Vol. I: How to Overcome a Poverty Mind-set
Vol. II: How to Move into God's Financial Blessings

There are fundamental changes you can make in the way you think which will help you release God's blessings. This is a balanced look at the promises of God with practical steps you can take to move into financial freedom. It is time for Christians to recapture the financial arena. These two volumes will inspire and create faith in you to fulfill God's purpose for your life.

Other Books by Harold R. Eberle

God's Leaders for Tomorrow's World
(Revised/expanded edition)

You sense the call to leadership, but questions persist: "Does God want me to rise up? Do I truly know where to lead? Is this pride? How can I influence people?" Through an understanding of leadership dynamics, learn how to develop godly charisma. Confusion will melt into order when you see the God-ordained lines of authority. Fear of leadership will change to confidence as you learn to handle power struggles. It is time to move into your "metron," that is, your God-given sphere of authority.

The Complete Wineskin
(Fourth edition)

The Body of Christ is in a reformation. God is pouring out His Holy Spirit and our wineskins must be changed to handle the new wine. Will the Church come together in unity? How does the anointing of God work and what is your role? What is the 5-fold ministry? How are apostles, prophets, evangelists, pastors, and teachers going to rise up and work together? Where do small group meetings fit in? This book puts into words what you have been sensing in your spirit. (Eberle's best seller, translated into many languages, distributed worldwide.)

Church History,
Simply Stated

How did the Church get to where She is today? How did we get so many denominations? Who are the leaders who formed our thoughts? Where is the Church going? To fully answer these questions requires a knowledge of the past. Here is a simple, concise explanation of Church history. With two or three hours of reading, anyone can develop a clear picture of our Christian heritage.

Other Books by Harold R. Eberle

The Spiritual, Mystical, and Supernatural

The first five volumes of Harold R. Eberle's series of books entitled, Spiritual Realities, have been condensed into this one volume, 372 pages in length. Topics are addressed such as how the spiritual and natural worlds are related, angelic and demonic manifestations, signs and wonders, miracles and healing, the anointing, good versus evil spiritual practices, how people are created by God to access the spiritual realm, how the spirits of people interact, how people sense things in the spirit realm, and much more.

**To place an order
or to check current book prices:**

Web Site: www.worldcastpublishing.com
E-mail: office@worldcastpublishing.com

509-248-5837

Worldcast Publishing, P.O. Box 10653
Yakima, WA 98909-1653

On-line Bible College:
Institute for Hope and Life

- Study at home
- Earn a certificate, Associates degree or Bachelors degree
- Study and proceed at your own rate

- Several courses taught by Harold R. Eberle
- Many other outstanding instructors from Vision International Education Network.

http://instituteforhopeandlife.com